LONDON'S PRINTS

Written by: Kieona L.R. Fairley
Copyright © 2018

While immersed in the dark, your footprints brought me to the light. Your still and lifeless body resurrected me. To my son London, may your footprints touch the hearts of others. May our story confirm there is life after loss. This book is dedicated to my two beautiful sons London, and Micah Exantus. Thank you for teaching me how to love and live again. Although you could not leave your footprints here on earth you have left your prints in many of our hearts!

London Kyrie Exantus
12-5-2011

Contents

BROKEN…ART

In my space of what seemed to be brokenness, I found writing. When it appeared that pieces of me, my innocence, and views of the world were destroyed, I found a way to piece myself back together. I realized that I could rewrite my own story, and that I did not have to follow those who came before me. Only through reading my thoughts, was I finally able to see this. The only way to get unstuck from my past chapters was to find the true me. I never was broken, never tarnished, or damaged goods. I am light, and through my writing I am able to display that. I am the letters and the combination of words spilled on the pages. A compilation of pieces, which when compiled together make a creative form of art. I write to make sense of life's nonsense. It is beyond comprehension. It is tuning in and vibrating with myself on a spiritual level. It is the becoming of a uniquely created masterpiece; broken art.

INTRODUCTION

It's easier to walk within your shadow as opposed to stand within your individual light. I was safe and comfortable in my darkness. Who would have known that a tiny set of footprints would have paved this path for me? I loved a soul that shared my breath, but he never got a chance to breathe on his own. He was whole, the purest form of love that filled my womb. Life is created in the darkness of the womb. I was loved, and was love, but my life on the outside made me question this. Every page in this book is my gratitude to the life of my son London Kyrie Exantus. Every page is every tear I cried, all the pain and anger I felt. Also, the wisdom and questions I have acquired along my journey of child loss, divorce, lack of self-love, and my return home. These emotions have been compiled into a series of short stories. My son in a way sacrificed his life here on earth for both of his parents. It took me to experience such trauma to wake up and realize that I wasn't living. By means of living my life to its fullest potential, living in love, and living a life without fears. I have seen a grave yard full of abandoned dreams, Oak Grove Cemetery was a place I became a frequent visitor. Dec 5, 2011, I gave birth to the death of a dream.

I was required to endure the pain and physical work of giving birth to my child that was deemed already deceased. I was forced to experience the balance of life; both darkness, and light, like a solar eclipse at 3:56 pm. I was able to experience what could have been, to kiss, smell, and dream again. I was forced to be amongst rooms filled with new mothers and their new babies. While the new mothers tried to figure out how to silence their newborn's cries, I waited to hear, or feel anything from my stillborn son. He was exactly what I felt, lifeless and numb. Imagine being forced to put in work, physical and emotional investment into something that was already dead. A mother's dream that was tarnished, a dream that ended way before it began. Most people fear failure, but at that moment I feared nothing within the physical realm. They say that death comes in a group of three, don't ask me why I have no clue. I guess I was the third. I no longer feared death, as I have died spiritually three times in this lifetime. First, being the loss of my son, then my marriage, and finally the loss of self. Not a physical death, but a spiritual death.

Spiritual death is when the pain permeates the soul. Physical death leaves behind scars and last temporarily. It most likely affects the loved ones more than it affects the individual transitioning. Spiritual death is when the pain permeates the soul. My mother used to ease my fears of physical death as a child, by reminding me that death is something we most likely won't remember. She would always ask me "Do you recall the very moment you were born and how, you will leave this world just like you came in it." I found comfort just like many individuals in the idea that some events will be forgotten. I would not be aware of what actually was occurring during my physical transition.

Why did no one ever tell me about the death of the soul? This is the death that occurs here on earth. The one many people physically wait unconsciously to transition unto, due to the emotional pain from their realities they have created. I have seen loved ones experience this spiritual death, only to remain in the very chapters in their life where their soul was damaged. You know how in the scary movies there would be ghost they described as having unfinished business. These are the people who have experienced spiritual deaths. Staying in the same chapter where they spiritually died. Spiritual death to me is by choice. It is a mental and emotional suicide. You are physically present and are capable of completing your daily tasks, but you have chosen to give up on life and your dreams.

In death, I found my voice. I spent most of my life invisible to society and to myself. My vessel roamed this earth but my spirit and soul died that day. The only people that could see me were those who truly loved me or considered me important. I slowly gathered pieces of self through being validated by others determining my worth, and by the success I have acquired along the way. By doing so, you give up your will to live. The interesting thing about darkness is that it is fed by fear. In fear, it multiplies creating disease, pain, hate, and depression. The darkness, when spoken of, can be perceived in a literal term with people looking for its physical aspect. The darkness I mean is one that is internal. It is the cloud that shifts the perspective from our natural joyous state. Darkness is the tainted ego, the very perspective that provides a storm over every situation you may experience. That darkness creeps its way into those in a vulnerable state. The very individuals that lose their sense of innocence, or experience an event so traumatic, that it separates them from the rest of society. That darkness grows within us in solitude. In solitude we are in our own heads, and create a dysfunctional reality due to our clouded perception.

It took me a while to move beyond my fear and to escape my darkness, as it appeared many of my loved ones were also comfortable within theirs. The inequity and generational pain ran through my veins and was imprinted on my DNA. We talk about life being unfair but what about those who were created from a tainted love. One from a lack of understanding of what true pure love is. I was created out of darkness, addiction, lack of self-love, and feelings of unworthiness. I have fought for my freedom and my belief in something different. Escaping to free yourself from your own chains and the chains that have been placed on you can be very ugly. It is a form of slavery that seems impossible to breakaway from. It appears that everything around you has set you up to fail. A life predestined for struggle and pain. It's unfortunate but it took me to lose my first child to awaken. What happened to me by no means does it define me, but it has allowed me to tap into my own spiritual desires and has lit the path for me and my living son Micah. When trauma occurs you can choose to have a breakdown or a breakthrough. Everything that occurred up until that moment weighs of no value. Things that used to be entertaining are no longer amusing anymore. Your relationships with others shift as you have different desires and reasoning for your relationships. Every degree, job, money, or any material thing becomes irrelevant. Material things like a house don't feel the same anymore when a person that helped to make it a home presence is gone.

I have felt every emotion you could feel in the span of twenty-four hours of being in that hospital room, after giving birth to my deceased son. He may have physically left this world, but he spiritually lives on through us. Energetically we are connected as there is a cord beyond the umbilical cord, and the experiences both positive and negative contribute to our spiritual evolution. There is a very popular Christian poem called "footprints" about a man that started his journey with two sets of footprints in the sand. During the darkest times in his life he noticed that there was only one set. Throughout this time he believed that God left him to walk alone, but came to realize that was the time God carried him. It took me six years to complete this project, as I had mixed feelings along the way. Much of the writing was completed right after the loss of my son, and some many years later. You will see a difference in maturity and understanding of my respect of life's balance.

I have come to learn that the Sun, and the Moon are both necessary for the universe to function. This also applies to us, as spiritual beings. I had to move from the "why me" and to gain a level of gratitude for the darkness I have experienced throughout my life. I had to understand that forgiveness like every other journey has no destination or end point. That pain which had been inflicted upon me from those I loved, were hurting too. My experience was necessary for me even to sit here and turn my story into this book. One tiny set of footprints was all I was left with. Dried ink on a white piece of paper with his time of birth, and the name of his parents. I received both a birth and death certificate the same day. I gave birth to a dream, and planned a funeral the same day. Dec 5, 2011 the woman everyone once knew, and the woman I thought I was, died with London (my son). My state of consciousness shifted as I became more aware of being fully present. Everything that I had been taught up until that point, I began to question. I was far from HOME. My core foundations and beliefs needed to be reprogrammed. I had absolutely nothing left to give to anyone, including myself. Until one day I choose to live my life fully, for the life my son was unable to live.

I recently took a late night trip to the ocean. I decided to let go of the last few items I had that belonged to him. I was given a box with his blanket and strands of his hair. You never fully realize your level of healing, until you push yourself to the point you are uncomfortable. Since Dec 5, 2011, I have carried his box along with me to every home I occupied. There was a sense of guilt for me, as I wanted him to know that he was loved. I felt like I never got the chance to tell him that. Not a day goes by that his name does not cross my mind or he is not in my prayers. Items hold energy, and that box was filled with the energetic emotions of me, his father, and our family from that day. I chose to let go and make room for new. The ocean seems endless and is another world on its own. Water is scientifically known to carry emotions and intentions. My intent that day was to let go of the pain behind my story, and begin to use it to inspire others. I placed the box in the ocean not knowing how much I was emotionally attached. I cried and prayed to the heavens, but I knew this was best for me and my evolution. With my presence on the beach and my feet grounded within the sand, all I could hear was "welcome home mommy."

Home is not a place, it is a feeling, and for most of my life I have been so disconnected from my inner being. Home is the core version of my total being as a spirit, living within a human experience. The moment you find yourself is the moment when you have lost everything you defined yourself by. As a woman, I defined myself as what I did and who I did for. I have discovered that I have a greater purpose outside of that. Only through self-love will I be able to fulfill this purpose. For so long, I have searched for home. A place where I felt I belonged, accepted, loved and family. Now I realize that home has always been within me. Like the ocean, it requires me to be vulnerable, in tune with my emotions, and aware of the balance of darkness and light within life. Through my healing journey, my son Micah is able to have a clear path set for him. Only through my journey of self-love will he see how to love himself. Learning is primarily through experience and observing, not through what we say. Join me on this journey of love, pain, anger and finding peace. Welcome to London's prints.

FREEDOM OF SPEECH...

In both death, and within my darkness, I found my voice. Freedom of speech; words both written and spoken are powerful. Words can enlighten you or discourage you. Build you up or bring you down. Words attack both your physical and mental. Painful words can pierce through your heart and reside in your mind. Leaving memories of one's words spoken. Speak your mind, but train your loose tongue. Evaluate your thoughts before spoken, once said is once done. You can't place a band aid on a wound in a heart. You can't erase a mental scar

LOVE LOST…

Love began when love was lost…When love was found… that's when I began to understand its true meaning, and realize it really never left.

OCEAN...

The ocean is my sanctuary. The place I would go to escape my reality. I always wondered what my connection to the Ocean was, and now I know. The salt water is cleansing to the spirit, and the beauty is calming. While staring at the ocean, it appears to have no end. This represents the lack of a destination within this life. The opportunities of what may be on the other side are endless. The body of water provides, and supports many different forms of life. As peaceful and serene the ocean may be, it can also be destructive. When storms hit, the waves can be tragic to those that dare to swim its waters. That once beauty can be destructive to all that it encounters. In life there needs to be balance. To better understand and appreciate the beauty of life, we have to embrace the good and the bad. The reason I chose the photo of my son running on the sand for my book is because what the photo represents. As humans we always want answers or proof of things. We need something tangible, something the five senses can experience. The photo I chose for the book represents a time in my life where I thought I walked alone. My son in the photo represents the plans God had for me.

The ocean represents the peace and calm after the storm. An ocean with no end, that represents the life I have built for my son. My evolution of healing was not only about me, but it provides a safe space and a place of love for my son's life journey. In the photo it appears that he is alone, but I was right behind him snapping the photo. In his life, I am positioned in that very spot to let him know I will always be there. Like the poem "Footprints" my son has love surrounding him. Love surrounding him physically on this earth, and those that have spiritually passed on. I am learning to trust God and my spiritual guides, to lead me on the right path. What I have learned will be passed on to my son as well. He represents a new generation. He represented the generation of renewal and breaking of old beliefs. The title London's Prints are because of the uniqueness of humans prints. My stillborn son is responsible for opening my eyes. He has led me on a journey of personal healing and building for his brother Micah. Everything I do, and everything I see, has meaning. All that I have left of him is a set of footprints, but those very footprints led me on the path I am on today.

SUN AND MOON...

We didn't see eye to eye on many things but the ocean was not one of them. I was the Sun, and he was the Moon. During the sunset, when the moon would rise over the ocean, this was the only time we would connect. We would only connect when the ocean was between us. A lot of people are not aware of this side of us, but water brought us closer together. One of our first dates was at Lake George, and we spent many summers on beaches all over the east coast. The Sun and the Moon are rarely out at the same time as they both had different purposes. So did we. We would spend hours on a beach soaking in the rays of the sun, and being cleansed of the salt water. Every dip in the ocean our connection was reborn. We were free to be ourselves, free to be in love. Our ocean visits allowed us to put our differences aside, our differences and reality behind. The ocean reminded us of how we fell for each other. Two different souls, from two different worlds coming together for the purpose of love. The very thing that united us was a reminder of the good and bad in all. The moon provides us with light, just not as bright as the sun. Does that make the moon any less important to the universe?

AVANT LONDON

PSALM 23

The Lord is my shepherd; I shall not want.
He maketh me to lie down in green pastures: He leads me beside the
still waters.
He restoreth my soul: He leadeth me in the paths of righteousness for
His name's sake.
Yea, though I walk through the valley of the shadow of death, I will
fear no evil: for Thou art with me; Thy rod and Thy staff they
comfort me.
Thou prepare a table before me in the presence of mine enemies:
Thou anoint my head with oil; my cup runs over.
Surely goodness and mercy shall follow me all the days of my life: and
I will dwell in the house of the Lord forever.

AMEN...

I was once told that there are three biblical scriptures assigned to me, Psalm 23, 51, and 91. Every night before bed, my son and I say Psalm 23. Psalm 23 is a comforting prayer that reminds us of God's protection and guidance. I was born a Christian; yet I don't consider myself any particular religion. I am inspired by the words and the sense of calm it provides. I still believe in GOD but my religion is Love. On my evolution, I have realized that a lot of the things we believe and do, are a result of us following the lead of others. Most people remain Christian or Catholic because that was a part of their upbringing. They participate in traditions that have been passed down for generations, some not even knowing or understanding the history behind it. As I evolve and flourish, I make it my responsibility to understand the words I say, and things I do.

What I mean by this is to research or get a better understanding of what I do, and why.

Recently, I responded to a member of the family's motivational post by saying AMEN. The post really touched my soul, and it actually reminded me of a sermon or something that a preacher would say. So what better way to respond than to say AMEN! Then I thought to myself, what does AMEN actually mean? I have been saying it all my life, whether in church or around family. It is the ending to every prayer, and is universal across most languages and countries. I had to figure out what was I truly saying.

After conducting some research, I have found that we have been answering our own prayers all this time. To pray is a form of meditation and the conclusion of AMEN is the confirmation. AMEN is originally derived from Hebrew meaning "so be it". "So be it" that the very circumstances that we face, regardless of their inconveniences or pain caused, is necessary to our passage. Saying "So be it" to me is a reminder to surrender. I have to constantly remind myself that it is not always up to me to find a solution. Many times while in difficult circumstances finding a solution out of temporary emotions can create more problems. "So be it" is a reminder to have faith that even through our times of trouble, we have to realize that everything is working out for our greater good. "So be it" is a reminder of the power of the present, being in the now, and minimizing your fears of tomorrow. You want change? So be it. That very thing you desire or wish to be. The change you wish to see in the world as well as the answers to your complications in your relationships, finances, fears and dreams. Your prayers require action from you.

So the next time you pray, pray for the strength to improve you. To create in you a pure heart, the ability see light within your darkness, to except the things you cannot change, and to understand that everything is purposeful. No matter what your current circumstance, listen to GOD speak through you as you say AMEN. Reminding you to live in the moment, love fully, and understand you are only in control of you. AMEN.

CINDERELLA...

Definition...
1. A Young woman with a lack of familial support. She is known to be a hard worker, but lacks direction in life. A kind soul that wants different from the life she was brought up in. She spends her life trying to clean up after others. Carrying the burden of others, and not enough time spent on personal dreams and goals. She is forced into adulthood with little guidance. Eventually she will find fairy godmothers, people that love like family along the way.
Cinderella was what some of my friends used to call me. A term they used to make fun of my adult responsibilities as a teen. I didn't understand at the time, but I realized I was different from my girlfriends. We all had different upbringings and different responsibilities. While many of them were just responsible for being a teen, I was worried about working and providing things for myself.

At eighteen, I was kicked out of my father's house over some chores not being done. I'm not going to lie; I was what adults would consider disrespectful. The only problem was they didn't realize me growing up so fast, led me to believe I was on their level. I called the adults out on their wrongdoings. I learned at an early age that just because you're older doesn't make you right. I was playing the role of an adult, while my friends were away at college. The interesting thing was watching them all after college. Graduating with degrees they wouldn't use and learning about the world, while I was doing everything backwards. I always had my own place, worked a full time job, and handled life on my own. I got a head start but did not always make the right decisions. I spent enough money on rent that I could have owned a house by now. I messed up my credit, because when mistakes were made, I could only rely on myself. There was no one to clean up my mess. I decided to write this because I know of a few young girls that fit this glass slipper. It may not look so pretty now, and no prince charming is going to save you.

My advice is to use the tools that you have obtained through the struggle to succeed. In your current circumstance you are being taught a valuable lesson, so pay close attention. You will have a gift of indescribable gratitude because you did it all yourself. Unlike the Cinderella in the story, when your time comes you will know how to keep it. You learn to be disciplined. There will be plenty evil stepmothers, and wicked step-sisters. There will be people who will try to bring you down. One day all your hard work will pay off!

IF ONLY YOU KNEW (PATTI LABELLE VOICE)…

She reminds me of Patti Labelle, or maybe that is the image I created of her in my mind. She loves to sing, cook, and spend time with her family. She had a voice just like her, before the cigarettes paid a toll on her vocal cords. I recall my father always bragging about her ability to sing. We recently had another fall out. There is always a constant misunderstanding between the both of us. She has the powerful desire to be respected, and my desire to be heard. Neither willing to provide either, but I have a platform that allows me to do so. She doesn't realize it, but I have already mourned the loss of her. I watched her die when I was a young girl.

The last argument she told me that I never have her back. If only you knew…They say growing up in a black household and being a young woman can be tough. Majority of the households are run by single mothers with very little presence from the fathers. A counselor once asked me did you ever feel loved by her, and the unfortunate answer is no. She used to always tell me when she was drunk, how her lack of affection began with her mother. She told me how she fell in love with countless men, but I never seen her love for herself. Had your back? Let's just say I have pissed in cups for her, with no clue what I was doing that for. Only to realize I was helping her with random drug test for her employment. The same company years later she got fired from. When tragedy hit our family in 1996, she died along with them. I recall cleaning up throw up from the side of her bed, and caring for my toddler brother while she partied the night away. Have your back? She had my grandmother, my cousin, and a tribe of women to call on for help, and childcare. Instead I played as her caregiver, and was screamed and yelled at when I desired for her closeness.

She was great at giving, as I had a shit ton of toys and material things. Just like my ex-husband, her affection and love was too costly. I recall panicking calling local bars, and hospitals, because she stayed out all night. I played mom at the tender age of 13. I barely passed middle school as I was being bullied at home and in school. I knew exactly the right time to ask her to sign my report cards. The night after she was drinking was the perfect time. She never paid attention. Her pain affected all of her loved ones. When she lost herself, she forgot about me. I found my uncle dead, had a seizure, and not once did anyone ask "are you okay?" Fuck therapy give it to God. Kieona is strong so she can handle it. I'm a writer today because of her. The only difference is I don't need liquid courage to be true to who I am. In a way, I feel like she has always disliked me because of that. She always taught me to be everything else except for myself. Be more cute and sexy like your cousin. She would constantly remind me to stay out of the sun "you're already black."

She taught me about toxic relationships and wondered how I ended up with a man like that. You my greatest teacher! I didn't grow up to be a "Dike" but I do embrace my masculine energy. I monitor my drinking because I never wanted it to take over me like it did her. My father may not have been any better but he did teach me how to be a woman. I learned from a man how to care for myself. You tell everyone that I choose to live with my dad, and you're right, I did. If you only knew, I made that decision because I knew if I stayed my soul would have died too.

I made myself responsible for picking up her pieces. Cleaning up after the mess she made. My teenage years were stripped from me. My mother allowed no room for me to make mistakes. She created enough hell in her own life that I did not want to add to it. I recall my cousin's mother the "known" addict of the family tell me there was no difference between the two. The only difference was my mother had a job. She was right. I was the disrespectful child because I exposed the shit she sprinkled with sugar. The exterior she worked so great to cover. She was a functioning empty soul. Where were you for all three graduations, prom, my two sons being born, and anything else positive that has happened in my life? If you only knew… that through your hell, you unconsciously dragged me through, yet I still loved you. Even through all the lies you have told about me as if I were your competition, and not your daughter. You raised me up to be independent and nurtured my brother. You tried to hurt me with the very demons you had dancing in your closet.

I gave you another chance. A second chance at bonding with my son. Even though he gets to see a different side of you, I still have not let my walls down. I don't trust you with my son for a sleepover or anything without my presence. I value his childhood and his perspective on love. I don't want you to teach him your conditional love. The love that is available only when you are pleased with one's actions. One in which subsides as soon as you are unhappy. I don't want him exposed to your intoxicated love. The emotions you spew with liquid courage that I hold onto, until the following day when you are angry and sober. Although life has changed for you because your body doesn't allow certain things, your heart still remains closed. I am not your competition, I am your daughter. You have abused your title as the walls I have built because of you, made me fear others on the outside. In a way, I believe you dislike me because of my strength. I see how easy it was for you to fall into the negativity as I have experienced everything you went through and more. If you only knew…beyond those men, beyond the drugs and alcohol, beyond your fears and insecurities, there was a little girl that truly loved you unconditionally. To the point that when she became an adult she encouraged her self-love journey to you as well. I found the secret and couldn't wait to share it with you. But your heart was not open. If you only knew…

UNCONDITIONAL LOVE…

Loving as a parent comes easy knowing the child is an extension of you. The true unconditional love comes when you realize that your child is their own person. Like with any other relationship, you have to commit to loving them as a whole. Those parts that are an extension of you, and the parts that is not.

LOVE...

LOVE...

      To lose love is like losing air. So close, so near to death. If we don't have air then how do we survive? Air is vital to every being here on earth. Without air we will die. LOVE is also vital to every being. Without love it will be the death of your soul. Love is an energy that does not die as a result of the loss of a loved one. This energy transcends beyond the physical realm. Love can be dangerous to those who abuse it. Just like a street drug for the first time, the high can leave you with a lifelong addiction. For me, love is my personal addiction. Just like most addicts, they try to fill some form of a void by using toxic things that can be detrimental to their health. My void is my personal battle with myself. I am constantly learning new things about myself as I grow older and I have a problem with loving myself. This is extremely important, as we all should know. I can't count how many times I have been told that I cannot love someone else if I do not love myself.

To a certain extent they are right. The only problem is I love too hard. I leave nothing for me, or so I thought. I give, and they take. Once the relationship ends I am left with a void, left unfilled and feeling incomplete. I swear after experiencing heartache, it's like I have to start all over again. I have to learn about me all over again. What are my likes and dislikes? Slowly crawling until I can walk again. The thing is though, once I begin to take my first steps and begin walking on my own. LOVE comes and knocks me down. I guess you can say I relapse. I become dependent on my spouse to give me my high. Once they stop, the energy is withdrawn from my soul slowly. I am committed to breaking this cycle and dedicated to going into my next relationship whole.

I WOULD NEVER...

My pregnancy with London was not my first. It was actually my second. Both were unexpected, unplanned, both tragic. Only my first was from my first real long-term relationship and it was terminated. I had an abortion at six weeks pregnant. I thought that getting an abortion would be the best answer. My relationship was on the rocks. I was in school and working, just starting to figure shit out. It was definitely a selfish act on my part as I look back on it now. I had my own apartment, although with a roommate. I was about 21 or 22 years old. The very few people I confided in, made my situation seem as if it was the end of my current world. I was told there would be no life after that. My boyfriend at the time was cheating, and was more concerned about his own issues. The problem was I never thought that I could get pregnant. Here I was with this guy for five years, and I never even had a scare. I was never an avid birth control user, and figured hey if it happens, it happens. Well it did!

I remember it like it was yesterday. I was working like crazy as a certified nurse's assistant at a nursing home facility. I remember going home to my huge bachelorette pad; I shared between a childhood girlfriend of mine. I had kept an agenda constantly marking my period start and finish days on the calendar. So I knew that I was to be expecting my cycle soon. That particular day, I was having cramping as if my menstrual cycle was about to begin. I remember putting a pad on to protect myself if Mother Nature had decided to sneak up on me. The following day I had spotting, so I thought I was in the clear. Only to notice it completely stopped a few days later. At this point I understood my body was going through some sort of change, and I needed to find out what it was exactly. At this point I decided to purchase a pregnancy test in which the results were negative. Within a span of three days, and three other pregnancy tests I received all negative responses. With the confusion, and all the stress, I just figured Mother Nature was running on her own time. Instead of trying to self- diagnose, I decided it was time to take this issue to my physician.

At the doctor's office, who at that point was still my pediatrician, I was given a pee test. This test also indicated that I was not pregnant. I knew that there was something else that needed to be done, so the doctors decided to draw blood for the lab. This is the most accurate, especially when it's too early to detect HCG levels in the urine. It takes four weeks for the HCG levels to be in a certain range for you to get a positive test result on home pregnancy test. About three days later, while working a 7-3 shift, I remember getting a call on my cell phone from my pediatrician. My stomach was in knots and my hands extremely sweaty as I waited for her to tell me the results. I stood by one of the huge windows that had a view of the staff parking lot. Pacing back and forth the pediatrician said the test was neither positive nor negative, and decided I needed a few more days to retest. So I just took the situation in my hands and figured I will wait a week and then try another pregnancy test. I remember the day that I got the positive I was in utter shock. I could not believe it. Things do happen when you least expect it. My boyfriend and I at the time discussed having children, but nothing ever happened. At this point in our relationship he couldn't even stand being around me. This was just the beginning of me realizing how God works on his own time. I was going through a ton of emotions, and happiness was not one of them. I never thought at this point I would still be working as a nurse's assistant. I wasn't making enough money to raise a child. I wasn't mature enough. I truly thought up every excuse in the book to persuade my decision .My mind was made up.

London's Prints

JUST WASN'T READY…

The days leading up to the abortion were hell. I slept my life away most of the time. I never had to experience morning sickness but raisin bran crunch cereal became an everyday meal. I guess you could say it was cravings. According to me, I wanted to be completely disconnected from this fetus. Normally I would do research or look up things about the procedure just so I could get a heads up. I think I called a few family members who had also gone through it and they assured me that everything would be okay. The day before going in, I had spent most of the day with my then boyfriend trying to mend our relationship. I discussed with him many times about how he had been treating me. At this point he was so far gone, and more in to himself that he couldn't see anything good in me. We have been arguing for months about the same girl, and same bull shit. He had a friend in high school that he was really close to but I guess they never really looked at each other in that way. Or so he said. I just knew things were different by the way he acted towards me. He would always pick

Page | 37

a fight and basically wanted to spend time with me when he wanted. I personally don't care what any man says but there are no friends for them of the opposite sex. I just remembered how he made me feel like I was the only girl in the world for years, and now just the sight of me annoyed him. I remember dropping him off at his house in my midnight blue brand new Honda civic. All I remember was being really frustrated talking to him. Nothing at this point in our relationship was getting through to him. I was the enemy because he wanted to do him. At that point, I was getting in his way.

On my way home I noticed that he had left his phone in the car. I remember when we never had cell phones, it was probably a lot harder to get caught cheating. I had a huge issue with wanting to play inspector gadget, when my intuition was clearly all I needed. I am going to say this now and probably repeat this later. Women remember if you feel like something is not right … it isn't! I was told constantly by his mother to stop searching for things, for you will find them. Well I did. I could barely pull up to the parking lot on the side of our building without grabbing for his phone. My stomach was doing flips I was extremely afraid of what I was about to see. I opened up his black sprint flip phone and went through every text message, and every picture. I found a photo of his high school "friend" naked. This situation just validated the importance of me going through with the abortion.

This is not the type of a relationship I wanted. I could not put a child in the middle of this foolishness. Some may call me selfish but in reality it was a decision that I had to make for myself. I just remember speeding back to his mother's house where I just dropped him off, to confront him about what I had just seen. I remember going in the house and making a typical "I'm pissed scene" right in front of his mother. We exchanged a few words. I don't remember word for word, but recall him shoving me out of the door. He denied everything that I had just seen. Now that I am older, I understand why he responded in the way he did. He was upset about getting caught. The other reason was he was disappointed in the decision that I had made alone. As he shoved me out of the house even with the tears in my eyes, I knew I had made up my mind. We were together for about four years around that time, and he started to stray away from the relationship. The closer I wanted to be to him, the more distant he got. During this time I had a few guys that I would talk to or look to for comfort. I had a void that needed to be filled, and neither the baby, nor he could fill. It was a void that had been missing since a child. A void that I had to fix, and fix alone

OPEN BOOK...

Within my pages you will feel a connection, because like you, I have made mistakes too. People tell me all the time that my life is an open book, but they fail to understand its purpose. The emotions and experiences within my pages may be a lesson for those whose pages have yet been written. My book is open for those who desire for more. Who yearn to be educated through other's experiences. I am an open book for guidance and direction. I am a tool for you to use. I am an inspiration to those who fear the judgement of others. I have many chapters written and many still unwritten. I now understand my life's purpose, through using my pages for healing.

FRONT PORCH...

Everything about that home screams family, but it's current physical state represent the status of our family...Broken. I want to purchase this home back from the state, because as a parent, I know how hard she worked to build a foundation for her children. She sacrificed her dreams for everyone else, and this is something she has taught me **NOT** to do. As a parent, we try to prepare our children for their futures financially, but a trust fund or home does not teach life's lessons. I was so disappointed seeing the home get sold, because I knew what she sacrificed just to obtain that. I learned from her to give my son the fundamentals or what I would call the "I teach you what I learned for you to aspire to be better and wiser than me" fund. Money does nothing for someone who is not emotionally stable and prepared to receive.

Anyone that knows my grandmother knows her love of the front porch of her home. It was a closed in porch that was shielded with glass. She observed her loved ones and life on the outside from this glass. It was her shield and her protection from people, and the pain they brought. She knew everything about everyone even before they told her. She gave up on life, lost her faith, and the house wasn't a home anymore. She lost her husband and two children all in the same year. Her pain and anger was misunderstood. All of the kids from the neighborhood feared her as she was the "Grinch" of the neighborhood.

The front porch became her protection and shield but it also magnified her fears. As her blood, I am taking it upon myself to break that shield and generational curse. I am shattering that barrier of glass and facing my fears. I am my grandmother, except I will use God as my shield. My faith has been tested on multiple occasions but he has remained as my shield and guide through it all. Get off the front porch and step outside of your comfort zone to experience the beauty of life. Ask yourself what have you chosen as your shield? Are you preparing for your blessings? Build your children to aspire to do more than you as a parent!

PLANTED

My Grandmother enjoyed planting. Every day you would find her outside digging, and planting things somewhere within the yard. I didn't understand why she would do so barefoot. I thought it was just a southern thing. She was actually grounding; tuning into the beauty of the universe. Planting seeds was her high. She would nourish, nurture, and tend to her plants. The last thing I was able to give her was a bouquet of fuchsia colored roses. This was my way to show my appreciation. While she was in the hospital, she was unable to care or serve others. Unfortunately, this was the first time she was able to focus on self. I wanted to show her the harvest from her planting. I was one of the seeds. As, I continue to grow, I truly hope she is able to see the results of the seeds she has planted.

RESURRECTION…

The greatest love story as it is told is Jesus and the crucifixion. I usually don't like to talk about religion because it's such a controversial topic. However, it is fitting because the loss of my son was a test of my faith. I have experienced loss at such an early age. It all began when I found my uncle dead at the tender age of eleven. Not only was I going through puberty, and trying to find my way through middle school. My innocence was broken, and I carried my uncle's passing as a fault of my own. My uncle died of an asthma attack. Similar to my stillborn son, who never took his first breath, my uncle struggled to breathe. I blamed myself for not responding quickly enough because I heard the loud noise. When I found him he was under his bed unresponsive and foaming at the mouth. No adults were home at the time, and I was afraid to act. I was not taught how to handle this kind of situation and did not know CPR at the time. That entire year or maybe two, I carried the burden of what if. I did the same thing when it came to London's birth/death. What if I went to another hospital? What if I didn't trust the physician's word? What could I have done to not allow this to happen? The answer is nothing!

During these trying times my faith was tested. Who is God and why would he allow me to endure such trauma or pain? I know he knows my heart, so why would he have me confront these situations? I have screamed at God on multiple occasions in anger, as I never understood what he wanted from me. Still until this day his answers may seem unclear, but I am more aware of his intentions. He has built me into this warrior, his own private soldier. I recall going to church as a young girl with my grandmother and I disliked everything about it. I remember the pastor asking for those who wanted to be saved to approach the altar. I remember feeling so guilty when they would repeat the importance of asking God to come into your heart. As a young girl, I always had this intuition or acknowledgement that I was different. I have a pure heart and no matter how much I asked God to change it, he never fulfilled this wish. I would think in my head as the pastor was speaking, I knew God was already a part of me. I really was thinking if having God in my heart meant for my body to undergo convulsions as if I were having a seizure...I was all set! Now as an adult, and after having my faith tested, I am clear about this process. You may not agree with me but this is my perspective. Asking God to be in your heart is you seeking self.

What I mean by this is, you are God's child. You are made in his image and are the very piece of him. When you are on a path to seeking out the best form of oneself, you are seeking out God. This process is written out for you in the bible with the crucifixion as the example. When you are seeking out your passion, your life's purpose it requires uplifting of all areas of your life. This includes the physical, mental, and spiritual being that makes you. This process requires dedication and is a lonely path because you are the only one accountable for your life's path. Not everyone around you is going to understand and you are going to lose many followers. Look forward to your resurrection. I am not that fearful little girl anymore. I have endured so much death and pain in my life that I could only choose to live. I face today with the excitement of a toddler, looking forward to what God has in store for me. Endure the pain of the crucifixion today and prepare for your resurrection tomorrow. You'll know when you there because you will be the talk of the town.

UGLY…

"You sho is ugly" one of the famous quotes from the movie "The Color Purple". There are plenty of days that I feel this way. I constantly struggled with my image. Better yet, I struggled with others perception of me. My dark skin and wide nose were considered flaws in my youth. I have been compared to Whoopi Goldberg (Celie from the color purple) or on my good days Kelly Rowland. I recall my ex mother in law telling me that I'm like Michelle Obama, not the prettiest but I clean up very well. Don't be fooled by the Facebook post or my Snap chat pictures because it takes a lot of work to look like that. No, I don't wake up like this, and yes makeup and filters can sometimes be my best friend. It all started at home, I wasn't feminine enough and my mother reminded me that I would have to be the type to wear makeup to be pretty. I was also told that I would be the type to get married; I was semi-cute and very domesticated. I actually believed this because it came from someone who loved me. I learned earlier on that the words of loved ones stick, even when they can be poisonous.

My father, Mr. GQ himself, I would cry to, because I adored his skin complexion. I asked him if he thought I was beautiful and he always replied of course. I denied his affirmation, because he was my father, he was supposed to tell me that. I was a dark-skinned girl who had the nicest curl pattern that was damaged by a relaxer at an early age. To them, I spoke like a "white girl" and had white girl mannerisms. My body type athletic and I envied my cousin because of her curves. I wore training bras in High school, so the girls you see today were non-existent (referring to my boobs). I used to pick my friends like a girl would pick out clothes, whatever looked good to me. Choosing girls that I thought were attractive or what I wish I was, and not by substance. I battled with acne and until my twenties I really didn't gain my own sense of feminine style. I am far from perfect and society's standards are really making women way too hard on themselves.

I am not a bad bitch with a small waist and a big backside; however, I have a lot to offer. My skin absorbs the sun and glows just right. My eyes are my best feature personally to me.. One minute I may pack on a few pounds but when I'm ready I can snatch my skinny body back. Oh and the legs! I hear it all the time, Mrs. Turner, yes Tina you have nothing on me. Over the years, I tried to find ways to enhance myself to prove to others that I wasn't what they thought I was...UGLY. I looked in the mirror and fought with myself over the things others used to say, only to realize their opinions didn't matter. Now, when I use my makeup and get dressed, I use that to enhance how I feel inside. I use it as a way to express the person within. There are so many people out here that spend so much money on the surface but not investing in what is within. I have had guys that I was interested in tell me I'm too dark or that my curls were only for the "Spanish women". No, I do not take you telling me I'm "pretty for a dark skin girl" as a compliment either.

I recall going to Madrid with some classmates and they were all younger than me. They were all in their junior year, so about early twenties. They stayed in the dorms and were college students, so you could only imagine what their wardrobe consisted of. I was getting ready to go out and got a knock on my hotel door. The girls wanted to come but they weren't "club" ready. I spent 45 minutes making these girls up. Almost each one of them cried. They did not know they could look like that. I felt like I showed them a side I see in them. Feeling good comes from inside and is portrayed outward. I no longer dress ugliness or emptiness; I enhance and exude the person within. So just in case you were wondering about the glow...

DEPRESSION IS BLACK...

Black is defined as the "darkest color owing to the absence of or complete absorption of light." Black represents darkness and negativity; it is the absence of light or positivity. Depression is black and effects people of color daily. I am what they refer to as black, a title that was given to us to permanently cloud us from the light within. We as blacks don't call it depression; we like to use the word struggle. As I became an adult, and became responsible for my own understanding of life, I realized it is a mindset. Depression is an internal fight of good vs. evil and heaven vs. hell. An internal fight that we create and carry through our genetic predisposition and it ignites with our environment. Depression and negativity can suck the life out of you and the will to live. It is an energy that focuses on the lack that attracts more of the lack. It is the energy that focuses on fear and pain of the past. Depression, that negativity, is a silent killer within our community. It amplifies the feelings of unworthiness, and dreams are shattered. High blood pressure, diabetes, reproductive issues, mental health issues, and poor self-care/love are all physical signs of an individual's battle. They say it requires more energy to frown than to smile. We have to remind ourselves that we are the creators of our own destiny. Not where we come from or who was responsible for loving us. The church teaches people that God is in the sky or outside of us. I believe God and the light is internal. Tap into your light and remind yourself of your life's purpose. Regain that fearlessness and love we had as a child. Love and light always prevails but if you feel like you're losing the battle to negativity, seek help. Depression affects people of all cultures and colors especially black.

A LETTER TO MY FATHER...

Dad,

Or maybe I should refer to you as Courtney, because the term doesn't seem fitting. Iyanla always says, if you want to see the ending, look at the beginning. You set the tone for the men in my life hence the luck I've had in relationships. My first love was with a man who didn't know his father or love himself. You are the reason I give people so many chances. You changed. You changed on your own time after suffering from alcohol and drug addiction. You changed after loving my mother with your broken love, only to give other women the love she deserved. You gave up an addiction and learned to dress up your truth, and to conceal your darkness. You gave up being a parent, because you never really had one. There are six children of all whom have different mothers besides two, who experienced love with you part-time. I'm going to be honest, I always felt like you were doing what you had to. As opposed to doing what you wanted. I felt like a burden, your love for me was unique but definitely not unconditional.

I did everything I could to make you proud of me. How could you not see that I yearned for your attention and affection? I lost my first-born son, have a four-year old, and you were never present. But how can I expect you to be present for me, when you're not present for yourself. The pain of your past haunts you because you have not chosen to heal your past wounds. I recall the day the nurse attempted to draw your blood. She was flirtatious and excited to have an attractive patient to draw. The conversation ceased as she realized the difficulty to draw blood from your veins. Your skin healed but underneath the abuse of your veins remained. Only a professional would understand why. Your surface was clean, but underneath you poisoned your seeds with the pain of your past.

Your broken love and lack of self-knowledge has affected me as a 32-year-old woman. The karma you created set the tone for my life, only difference is I plan to fight. I married you! You couldn't stand my son's father, but he was a reflection of you. He was a lost soul hurting women with his broken love. He also dragged others through their emotions while trying to find self. .Each man I have dealt with carries some symbol of you. The abandonment, emotionally unavailable, and the "I'm not there yet but I will be back when I am". You planted six seeds in cement. Each seed you planted only having a piece of you part-time. You are alive but never stood up for me, let alone walk down the aisle to give me away to a loving man. You are the reason I continue to find men who fall short of my basic needs as a woman. Every man who I encounter tells me that they can't give me what I need.

My insecurities bring me back to that little girl who wanted the emotional connection with her father. She wanted a man to show up. She needed a man to be present. Out of all the women in your life, I genuinely loved you. My mother didn't understand why, but it's a bond between a father and daughter. You loved me the only way you knew how. I know now that I don't have to accept that from men. I can love them but not accept the love they are willing to give. It has been years since we have spoken, and the seed you planted in the cement is struggling in love to flourish. Your grandson saved me.

Where you and other men have left me wilted, he unknowingly waters me. Your children are what sustain you. They give you a sense of purpose. I don't understand why you would shut them out. I have learned to live without you. I'm all set with part time love. Children should not have to ask for love. Human contact and love is proven to help children grow. This was denied to me by you because of what you were taught. You were my first love, the one responsible for showing me love, and you left me heartbroken. My beginning will not be my end because I am aware of the pattern. I am breaking though the cement, and the cycle of broken love. I now know how to love from a distance.. Just know that through all your flaws, your pain, and your past...your little brown girl always loved you!

MY LETTER TO BLACK MEN...

Dear Black Men,

I apologize, for I was not taught how to love you. They say men and women speak different languages causing misunderstanding and conflict. The black men I knew and thought I loved, barely had a voice. My personal wrath and anger towards the other black men before you, I carried into the relationship with you. To be honest, the anger and hurt ran through my blood, because of the pain my father caused. I have seen the anguish and lack of faith my mother had in you. The "Good Black men" were the ones that were exclusive to white women. Don't even bother because a dark skinned girl like me would never stand a chance at least that is what I was told. I expected you to love me, when the world around us teaches you not to love yourself. We as black women don't have it easy either, but for you, there is no support. I can't I expect you to be the man for me, when your own father neglected this very responsibility. Your mother could only do so much between trying to provide, raise, love and support you. That job is meant for two.

My love was broken, sometimes possessive, and jealous. The things the bible tells us love isn't. Your behavior is only a reflection of how you view yourself. The immature thought of the more women you sleep with, is what the hood defines as a symbol of being a man. Little did you know that with that increasing body count, you shatter into smaller pieces. Your spreading of your broken love creates a domino effect of broken hearts. You were taught not to cry, that was the building blocks to your emotional unavailability. You never learned how to handle your emotions. You create children with women whom you don't see any future, hoping to be more than your father. Only to turn around and repeat because to break the cycle requires another level of strength that you believe you don't have. I had faith in you, the black man. More faith in you than you had for yourself.

I don't know how many times you have heard "He ain't shit". The confirmation of what you are starting to believe yourself. You pull away not to neglect the ones you love, but to find a way to fix things. It is in your blood to provide but your past hinders you from doing so. You drown your sorrows away with Hennessey and smoke until your troubles disappear. The black woman you chose, the one that was once your peace, has become the voice from the outside. She is not content with your trying, nor can she see beyond her frustration. We are both fighting for the same thing. We are looking to each other to fill avoid that our parents should have filled. I'm searching for the unconditional love of my father, and you the guidance and love of your father. Love is something we are born with, but how we show it through actions is a taught behavior. My only idea of a healthy relationship was what I saw on TV. It's not like that here in the real world. Black love doesn't have to be about struggle but generationally our bonds and foundation have been broken. Change is required when we feel like we are falling in the same space as the ones before us. As a black woman, I vow to heal my wounds and prepare for a better me. Hopefully I can inspire you to do the same. Deep down we both know we deserve and want something different. Dear Black man, help me break this generational curse.

THEY SAY OPPOSITES ATTRACT…

Before Having London I was in a completely different place in my life. Possibly the most confused I have ever been. Prior to London's conception, I was in a place that I thought I would never be. I was a rebel, and doing things that were against my morals, and against what I stood for. Many things that today, I am not particularly proud of. All my life, I can say I stuck to the rules. Honestly it was the guilt that I felt after. It felt like something was eating me alive. I let myself down. Or it could have been the fact that I did not want to disappoint someone. Constantly, I was fully aware of other's feelings but during this point in my life that all changed. I became selfish. My husband whom was my boyfriend at the time was incarcerated. I now know "never say never". He had got in to trouble. He was facing some serious jail time in which the charges were held in superior court. While awaiting trial he was incarcerated in a local correctional facility. Never in a million years would I have thought I would be in a relationship with someone that would end up in jail.

Here I was the girl who never even been to the principal's office, visiting her spouse in jail. I'm not too sure if it is true what they say as far as good girls liking bad guys. I wouldn't go that far. I do believe that opposites attract. My boyfriend at the time was the complete opposite of who I was in all aspects.

US...

I can recall the day that I met my now husband. I was living in the most amazing bachelorette pad with one of my childhood friends. Her name will remain anonymous. We were two young women in our early twenties and living pretty well off. I mean we were not rich, but we were living comfortably. Our apartment was huge with an old Victorian feel, in a historic part of the city. The ceilings were high and the rooms were huge. We didn't have the money to purchase amazingly expensive furniture. So we furnished the apartment with nice used items and made it fit our personalities. Although we were childhood friends, this particular person and I were opposites. Growing up I was the introvert and very insecure. She was more popular and very confident. We actually met when I was running home from the scene of an accident. My younger cousin was hit by a car. Her aunt followed me and brought her along to see if everything was okay. That day she had offered me some candy, and we had been friends ever since. My friend was every guys type. She had guys constantly wanting to date her. Many of them, if they were unable to capture her love, they would settle just being her friend. Some of her guy friends would come by and hang out. It was our place so we played by our own rules. She was more of the inside type, not much of a party goer like me. I can't help the fact that I love to dance.

The perfect night to me consisted of hanging at home with some drinks and friends. On this particular day, I just came home from one of my twelve hour shifts at the hospital and was getting ready to shower. When I had got in the shower, no one was there besides my roommate and I at the time. I recall getting out of the shower and opening the door to some guy sitting on the chaise lounge that was facing towards the bathroom door. There I was in my towel trying to scurry to my bedroom. I don't know how long I stood there in shock, but it was just enough time for me to realize that he tried to be a gentleman by apologizing. I wasn't really bothered because he didn't see much, but it did catch me off guard. Once in my room I was getting dressed to go absolutely no where so I figured I would hang out with my roommate and her guest. I walked in to the living room where I was greeted by my roommate and her two guy friends. They both seemed pretty young and both were really tall. I just remember seeing their legs sprawled across the living room floor from the futon they were seated at. I then sat on the chaise as my roommate began to introduce one of the guys who I have seen at the house before. A dark skinned guy with a baby face and low hair-cut. Although he was young looking he was extremely tall. The other guy was extremely thin, very thin for my taste. He had very distinct features as though he was a different ethnic decent other than African American. They both spoke.

We all just hung out and had some drinks while watching a movie or something. Once they decided it was time to go home, the thin guy had asked if he could get my number from my roommate. I guess he told her he was interested in getting to know me. My roommate knew that recently I just went through a relationship whirlwind with my last boyfriend, so she was skeptical on us getting to know each other. I had fun that night and never thought anything about another relationship, but little did I know that was the beginning of my relationship with my now husband.

He and I started talking on the phone and hanging out a lot. I was reluctant with other guys that I had met that summer after my five year previous relationship had ended. I was single for about a year and beginning to walk again .I was beginning to learn to love myself again, and now him. In my last relationship I had gotten so comfortable, that I had gained about 60 pounds. So when that was over, I had vowed to get myself back in to shape and back to the woman I used to be. I met a few guys along the way but at that point I hated love and hated men. Yeah, they were entertainment every now and then, but I couldn't let myself down again. "Hi my name is Kieona and I am a recovering love addict." That summer was fun filled, hanging out with my roommate and my new guy friends. They were young, silly, and care free. I remember my first conversation with him on the phone. I swear, I interviewed him like he was applying for a job or something. Honestly his answer to most of the questions I had asked should have been warning signs for me. Not signs that he wasn't a good man or couldn't be one. They were signs that he wasn't ready for me. I saw signs that his young soul was troubled. Signs that he was unaware of who he was, and could not be the man I needed. Signs I know now that I should have paid close attention to. They say you cannot be a man's priority, until he knows where he is going. At that time, he had no clue. "So what do you do for work?" I remember texting him. "I don't have a job right now" was his response. That should have been strike one. "Are you in school?" I sent in a return text. I know the job market has been pretty tight so I was not going to be judgmental. Plus he was still young, so I knew he had to be in school. "No. Not right now." he responded. Strike two. "Well what do you do or plan to do?" I asked. I was getting desperate. I wanted him to show me some sign of success or goals. I could tell that he felt the heat. He probably started to look at his responses as if this is sad. I need to be doing something with my life. What guy doesn't want to impress the new chick they are trying to date. To reignite my interest, he started telling me his plans or goal.

Things he eventually wanted to do. At that point, he passed the interview. We both did not have any expectations at that point for the relationship to go as far as it did. We both honestly thought it would be just a summer fling. At that point, he may not have had a job, but he was about to fill a position that probably was the hardest position he would have to fill. He would be filling that void in my life. He would become my new happiness, drug, and my new addiction. We were in the beginning of the most dangerous type of love. A love in which, I loved him, more than I loved myself.

Je t'aime plus que moi- même

THE HONEYMOON PHASE...

The honeymoon phase is the best. Those with love addictions like me; it is our first time high. Everything is new, and everything just seems so right. I swear we couldn't get enough of each other. You know the usual staying on the phone until one of you falls asleep, and calling that person as soon as they wake up. We did it all. One night, I went out with an associate from work to a twenty-one and over club in our down town district. This was our first time hanging out together and we were looking for a good time. The club was packed and the music just right. I remember having on a black bustier from Guess that cost me an arm and a leg. It was worth it though, because I looked amazing. My hair was in curls and my skin was glowing. I always love the look of my skin in the summer. It took me a while to feel that way about myself. I remember going to the bar to grab a drink and noticing him from a far. He was posted on a wall facing the dance floor. He was rocking his usual polo attire. I honestly think that is one of the reasons I fell for him. He was very clean cut. Trust me you would have thought he was an Ivy League student with his preppy style. I was extremely surprised to see him because he was too young to be in there. He was three years younger than me, so I had no clue how he even got in. I made my way to the dance floor to see what he was up to in an over twenty-one club. Really I was just getting him to notice me. That he did.

It was so nice to see someone so excited to see me and more enthused by the way I was dressed. I felt like Cinderella and he was my prince. At that moment he made me feel like the prettiest girl in the club. We talked and danced the night away. He had way too many drinks and was taking bottles from the bar. This was another red flag, but at the time I thought he was just having a good time. Little did I know that this was his usual behavior. I could tell by the friends he had, that they were the popular crew and had a reputation for partying, and girls. Some of the guys I have seen around the way. I knew there type.

That night I guess I was feeling a bit adventurous or maybe it was the two long island ice teas. I invited him back to my place. I had rode in with the associate from work, but told her I had a ride back. My house wasn't too far from the club. I could've honestly walked. I remember coming out of the club and complaining about my feet hurting. He had picked me up and carried me to the car. I don't know how, but I was much smaller then. He drove me home in his friend's truck at a speed he should not have been driving in residential areas. Thank God we made it to my house safe. I know what you're thinking, but it wasn't that type of night. I wasn't looking for a one night stand. I just wanted his company. Not only that but I do like to be cuddled at times. I'm sure it was difficult for him just to be invited over to cuddle; he was drunk and ended up passing out after our brief conversation. I remember undressing and telling him not to try anything. I don't like to sleep with clothes on so he would have to deal. We just laid there talking about relationships, and the things that we don't want. I remember telling him about my past relationship and how I don't want to be cheated on. He assured me that if I was his girl, that he would never do that to me. He also claims the same happened to him. We both had been hurt. We both wanted different. We both fell asleep.

ALL OR NOTHING...

My spirit was built with the understanding that with anything in life, I give it all or nothing. This has left me with heartache, confusion, pain and pleasure. I dive in head first into the unknown. If I only did this for myself, I wonder where I would be. If I gave myself my all, could I potentially save me, from me? My brain and heart are in constant uproar every day, competing for my attention. My heart always seems to win. At this point, I really have nothing to lose, but everything to gain. We expect consistency, but don't give to self, expect love but don't give to self. I've decided to give myself; my all or nothing.

HANCOCK...

I came to realize today, that I'm a screwed up superhero. Yes, I am the superhero that is aware of their capabilities to save others, but just haven't quite figured how to use it for good. I referenced Hancock as the title because I am him. I have a ton of personal issues but the power to change lives around me. I became aware of this superpower years ago, but have no clue when and where to exactly use it. I drink wine to ease my sensitivity to others emotions because I am an extreme empath. It helps me to tune out others emotions and problems just for the time being. When I decide to utilize my superpowers, the results are catastrophic. I am damaging to everything around me.

My superpower has become a burden as I have yet figured out the ultimate purpose. I am aware of my physical capabilities, but emotionally my special powers leave me feeling drained. My super power is love. Instead of defeating the bad guys, I try healing them with my superpower. This only leads to feeding their negativity and them obtaining their power over me. I become weak, left questioning my ability to defeat them. Fear is my handicap. It disables me to the point where I consider myself as "normal". I am in limbo, the point in which my abilities could either make me or break me. I have wished it away, and have had many sleepless nights. In my sleep, I fight to rest. I was called for something bigger but I was taught to think small. I am called to save others, but have yet to save myself. I am a superhero who has fallen. One who has been defeated and lost hope within self. Even though I am like Hancock, a natural superhero, who is going to save me?

CHANGE...

We are taught throughout our lifetime that we are not responsible for other's behavior; we are only responsible for self. Well yesterday, I had an epiphany. Gandhi said it best "Be the change you want to see in the world", but what does that really mean? Your job is not to sit and wait for others to change, you do so for self. You can't make someone change, however you can inspire them to do so. When you change, you promote, desire, and demand the same. You begin to attract the very things you give out. Your environment and the people around you will either conform, or leave you. When you begin to understand this, it will become easier to let go. The greatest gift is to share with others your trials and how you overcame them. Provide other with the resources you have obtained and the knowledge you have acquired.

Unfortunately most people are not aware there is different. They have become so used to their normalcy; they are unaware that there are levels to growth. I have lost many friends and family along the way. I still love them, but from a distance. My change affects all my loved ones around me. My advice is don't wait for that person, situation, or circumstance to change. Be like Gandhi, take control of your life and you be that change.

CORRECTIONS...

The most interesting part of my resume is my previous employment as a Correctional Officer. Yes, I was a Correctional Officer for a total of five years. I actually enjoy watching the interviewer's facial expression and sudden interest in my diversified employment background. Corrections? Really? My pleasant demeanor and personality confuses the interviewer as to how I fell into such a position. It was just that, I fell into an opportunity. Now that I think of it, I have played many acting roles with the uniforms I worn. None of the uniforms made me, they added pieces and skills to the person I am today. To be honest, the only two uniforms that fit me naturally are being a mom and a writer. Nothing was forced, it just came natural. My father, his brothers, my son's father, and many other men I knew had fallen in the system. Only they were wearing the opposing uniform. If it wasn't for my son's father, I would have never gone for the job. I was tired of working as a tech for the hospital, and CNA work on my free time. I wanted a career, something to fund my dream. The pay was great for a young woman my age, and so were the benefits. The thing that bothered me was what it represented.

A correction is an action or process of correcting something. As an officer, my job was to lead and correct behavior of grown ass men. As my fellow veteran officers would have called it, I was "Adult Babysitting". I was confused because most of the individuals that were responsible for correcting needed some corrections themselves. I was a black woman in a predominantly white male environment. The ones in orange looked like my father, my son's father, and my father's brothers. They looked like the friends I made in high school. Out of all the officers there were a total of 5 black staff members. There may have been seven, but a few of them didn't consider themselves black or not so much while in uniform. The institutions have this idea of minimizing recidivism but embrace the "job security" of the system that sets many for failure.

I was pregnant twice working for the jail, and that will be the last time my sons energy will be within that space. Don't get me wrong, there are people that deserved to be there because of the crimes they have committed. Majority of the inmates have mental health issues, which a jail is not the appropriate space for treatment (that's another topic). Jail to me represented purgatory. A place where individuals were able to choose between light or the dark. The reason I state that jail sets them for failure is because upon release they are released to the same environments. Same negative energies they have surrounded themselves around all their life. Many of them unfortunately don't know any better because of the generational ignorance. Me, I was their counselor. I gained my respect from being myself. That same personality was exuded to the offenders. I maintained this by not constantly reviewing their files or wrongdoings. Instead I met them for who they were at the point that I met them. I gave them the opportunity to build a rapport with me outside of their wrongdoings. Many of the officers had issues with respect I guess during their youth. They couldn't wait to put on a uniform to "correct" or become the exact same individual they had issues with. For me I saw both sides. I saw the frustration of the officers with the behavior they dealt with. I also saw that there was a reason behind the inmates doing, one in which we did not understand but was their truth.

Change is required to correct unwanted behaviors. Most importantly corrections should be made with the support of those who lead by example and with positive intentions. The world we live in today is one in which everyone is quick to judge. A world that is quick to find corrections for others, but none for themselves. We are all spirits that have a choice to choose between light or the darkness. Sometimes it requires someone to share their light to lead others out of darkness. Darkness in which they may not have known was a choice.

HEALING...

Time does not heal wounds, it changes your perspective. What occurred is an imprint. It does not determine who you are, but will be a factor in who you become. Healing has no sense of time, and every day is a day of forgiveness and rebirth. An opportunity to see your past through today's eyes, and the ability to foresight a better future.

INTOXICATED LOVE...

"A drunken mind speaks a sober heart" a saying that I've heard a lot but in so many different ways. A French philosopher came up with this idea due to his own alcoholism. I don't know too many people that can say they have never encountered this behavior from a loved one. Beyoncé called it "drunk in love". Chris Brown and a few other R&B artists called it drunk texting. Even country music tunes like Lady Antebellum "need you now" highlights this very statement. Scientifically, they say the reason for this is because the thought process is delayed. Intoxicated love is being emotionally available when they are under the influence. I'm not so sure of the exact history, but was told that the reason they call liquor/wine stores spirits is because there is a biblical significance. Under the influence their souls are free. Their words are unrestricted and carefree. The thoughts of you burst through their pride that will appear to them the next morning. They are as honest as a two year old, letting you know if they love you or hate you. Without the choice of drug they are stuck with the representative spirit. This is the spirit that you see every day, that lacks emotions. The anger and confidence is just a role to play, outside of their internal insecurities and fear of rejection. One glass, two glasses, a bottle...the spirit is free. The vulnerability and lack of judgment is no longer behind a cage. Sometimes the loved ones support the intoxication; because that's the only time they feel they are loved. If only they knew how to love you sober. If only they loved themselves when sober. What was once toxic, can turn into true unconditional love.

HE LOVES YOU, HE LOVES YOU NOT…

True love, pure unconditional love doesn't come and go with your behavior. Unconditional love overlooks your flaws. How can someone love bits and pieces of a whole you? His love is a reflection of how he was loved. By what he did and who he did for, not who he was. He loves you, he loves you not.

ACCOMPLICE...

He was physically incarcerated for the crimes he had committed. I was mentally, through my continued negative thoughts. All of these years I played the victim or as the innocent bystander to the death of my spirit. He committed the crime through his behaviors, while I consciously made an emotional decision to just sit back and watch. Powerless. In reality, and in my truth, I was an accomplice. The same thing that made him serve time, the same lies he told himself. He really believed that he was just along for the ride in that car with others of ill intent. Unknowingly, riding shotgun with a car full of individuals willing to commit a robbery. Associating with people that he knew were up to no good. Loving him, I did the same. I was riding shotgun to the crime, the death of my spirit, a robbery of my heart, and vision of myself. I was guilty, knowing damn well he had no sense of direction. I was an accomplice to the death of the old me.

.

RIDE OR DIE…

The longer I ride with you…the more my soul dies.

MOMMA...

I recently came across this situation with a friend of mine and have personally experienced it firsthand. This is a public service announcement to all women and young girls that are in an unhealthy relationship. If a man's momma says to you he is no good and you don't need to be bothered with him...RUN! As women we think too much, and in most circumstances people mean what they say. I have a degree in Psychology, so I am always over analyzing stuff. When his Momma tells you he is no good that is not translation for you are the girl to save him. It does not mean that she likes you enough to save you either. She is telling your ass to **RUN**!

I wish I would have had someone to tell me this when I experienced this, but every situation is a learning one. As a mother of a son, I have a real concern for the mothers who actually relay this information. First off, as a mother, my child (son) is a reflection of my parenting and if I have to warn you about him, what does that say about me? Second, I may appear to genuinely like you because I am telling you this, but what does this say about my character as a human being? Those same mommas that warn you about their son are the ones that support their "boyish" behaviors. This including the fact that his side chick has probably already met her and you are just another one of his victims. As a mother, I would not condone certain behaviors from my son and especially in my presence. As a momma, how do you feel going about describing your son in such a manner as if he was an ex that did you wrong? It all starts at home and at an early age! So if you're dating a guy and his momma says something to you about him being no good...*RUN*. She is giving you some valuable insight into what you're getting yourself into...firsthand.

SA MERE (HIS MOTHER)…

His mother wasn't aware or didn't acknowledge that her history was repeating itself through me. Her history reoccurred right before her eyes. She would always tell me he would have been different if she raised him. To some degree she may have been right. He may have had a little more respect for women, but their cultural beliefs looked more to finding love as a business opportunity. He came from a poor stricken country, so money was always an issue. They did not believe in marriage for love, it was more about marriage for opportunity. I couldn't imagine what it would have been like to go without eating, and being beaten by a parent just because they were angry. Love is placed on the back burner when basic needs are not being met. In my mind, I believe she still feels a sense of guilt for not being there during his childhood. This was the time he truly needed her the most. So she redeems herself through supporting him through both his good and bad. The same behaviors she left his father for she encourages and supports. We both grew up so differently. Our dysfunction and misguided ideas of love brought us together. His mother wasn't there physically during his childhood. Mine was gone emotionally.

EXPECTATIONS...

Why are we so backwards when it comes to setting expectations? Why do we wait until we are completely submerged in a relationship to set our "deal breaker"? It is okay to tell someone that you have particular needs and wants. If it is something they are not used to providing and would like to compromise then great! If not, you are to put your big girl panties on and make a decision. We all know from the beginning things that may be a personal "no go" for you when it comes to a spouse. Trust me you don't have to settle for what someone is offering. The fact that they are unable to provide certain things you require does not make them a bad person. They are just not for you! It's okay to tell someone you're dating what you need as an individual. For me personally I need someone that is attentive and a good communicator. These are just a few of the qualities that I require, but they mean a lot to me. At my age now, I am not afraid of losing a relationship. In this case ladies, it is okay to be selfish. Setting the expectations from the beginning will allow room for you both to grow keeping in mind each other's boundaries and expectations of the relationship. Don't get me wrong we change throughout the years, and so don't our wants and needs. One example that comes to mind is conflict between couples over having children. I swear for a while I was so against having another child, especially after my pregnancy and birth experiences. I am fearful, but also very cautious of selecting my child's father. If I was to meet a man who was amazing in so many ways but wanted a football team, I know this is something I do not want. Now if I went on with the relationship and avoided this expectation from my spouse, eventually this may create conflict within the relationship. You cannot change someone's mind about what they want and need out of life and a relationship.

Discuss your goals, dreams, and aspirations to see if you are both on the same path. I had to learn the hard way. I set my expectations when the "wrongdoings" occurred, and never left. I kept dealing with the deal breakers only to lead to heart-break and he lost all respect. Setting expectations is not just for your partner, it is an act of self-love. You are setting the standards of how you want to be loved, and sharing what is important to you. If they love you or want to be in your life your expectations will be important to them. Keep your expectations realistic; but don't settle.

YOU SHALL REAP WHAT YOU SOW...

They say that eyes are the gateway to the soul. The eyes can share things about a person without them telling you. I guess that explains why I can never look him in the eyes. I think I am afraid that if I do, that he could see right through me. I am very open with my life but there are still somethings that I don't want him to know. I know he is flawed and so am I. The whole story behind this "relationship" is a sin on its own. We both were wrong. Yet I still cannot look in his eyes. What am I truly afraid of? Am I afraid of my true feelings being exposed? This is something that neither did I want, or planned to happen. Now I understand why they say "never say never." Anything is possible. Please don't ever believe that it can't happen to you, because it will. I have morals and I have pride. I also believe that what goes around comes around. Although this is all true, when it comes to him it all goes out the window. I swear I did everything right up until this point. I never met a guy like him. Yeah, they are all nice in the beginning especially during the honeymoon phase. He was different. He saw me for me. He accepted me for my flaws and all. He saw me for how I saw myself. I always wondered if it was the age difference or the fact that he was experienced. He had done this before but not me. It was weird but this time it was different. I had a boyfriend, and he was married, another one of those things that I swore I would never. Life sure is funny. I never felt love like this…I wished he wasn't married.

MOM OR MAURY...

Falling in love with a married man was not a part of the plan. Matter of fact I discussed this with both of my parents. My boyfriend at the time was incarcerated and looking at potentially doing a lot of time. We just hit it off. It started with our love for music, and a few nights meeting at clubs after work on our days off. I confided in my mother who has experienced something similar, and asked her for her guidance. My father even met this man, and everyone loved him. I loved my boyfriend at the time, but wanted him to have the drive and personality of the married man. Only if I could build a man, like the popular children's store build a bear. My mother wasn't very happy about my choice, but my family really wasn't fond of my boyfriend and the way he treated me either. While pregnant with London, the married guy and I remained friends. In fact, there was a time when he was ready to risk it all, and leave the very life he knew. He was married with three children and I envied his situation. He had the American dream, but he still wasn't happy. We both connected like a match to a flame. It wasn't about the sex, but we truly were best friends. We both yearned to be loved, and we would provide that for each other. We both believed we were missing something in our current relationships. I now know it was the fact we lost ourselves by sacrificing so much of who we were, to make others happy.

I figured since I was respectful of his situation, then it wasn't that bad. I was "***respectfully disrespectful***". I did not call his phone, show up at his home, or start things up. I was actually okay with the love I got from being the other woman. This sounds weird with me just typing it. One day, my mother came to visit, which always ended up in some type of argument. My boyfriend was finally home, but so much had changed between us. My mother and I cannot be in a room for more than an hour before we disagree on something, but I always tried to make our relationship work. We got into an argument, and she felt compelled to tell my boyfriend at the time that my son I was carrying may not be his. I never once told my mother that. I couldn't believe that she turned my conversation with her about my relationship with the married man, to the fact that my boyfriend was not the father of my son.

My own mother! The sad thing about it was she until this day saw nothing wrong in what she said. I knew who the father of my child was, but it hurt me that my mother wanted me to hurt like she did. Interestingly, my brother found out the man he was named after was not his biological father. For years she kept this secret only for it to rear its ugly head as soon as my brother got older. She used her title as my mother to validate her anger towards me to bring further pain to my relationship. Hurt people, hurt people, this includes family. Since my mother said it, it had to be true. False. My boyfriend knew about what happened when he went away, and once he found out I came clean. He knew how much I loved him. I was wrong, but boy did I pay for it. I may have played the good girl role, while doing dirty deeds, but karma took notes, and returned the favor to me.

The married man lost a child as well. We shared a connection through our grief of loss, our children and ourselves. In the hospital after being checked in to give birth they gave me every medication under the sun to allow me not to feel. My boyfriend at the time stepped out to go and numb himself and I made a phone call to the jail. I don't recall the conversation but I just needed to connect. He understood my pain, and understood me. My boyfriend may have been there physically but with him it was emotionally. I forgave my mother, for she knew not what she was doing. She was emotionally bankrupt, and had nothing but pain to share with me. Her reality became mine and until my son's death did I realize, it was time to create my own.

LATE-NIGHT LOOKOUT…

When in love, we do some really stupid things. I felt compelled to write about this incident as the other day I laughed about it. The shit wasn't so funny when it happened. Life lessons… what stressed you back then will become humor to you years later. This is a hint and reminder that shit is not always as serious as we think. I wouldn't call it love it was more in a lack of love. Only those who feel insecure would act in such ways that I did that night. As I get older, I don't want to involve myself in situations where I have to seek the truth of a spouse. I rather go with my intuition and to the suspected culprit and seek the answer. There is no need for the extent that I went through to find what I already knew. The unfortunate aspect was that I was nine months pregnant. I was working at the jail in main security, with the primary responsibility to watch the cameras and answer incoming calls. It was another night of wondering what my son's father was up to while working the graveyard shift. I called him and he had the "I got an attitude because I have something I want to do" tone and clearly he did not want to talk. We were living in a fourth floor loft apartment with wood floors. I was ready to pop and deliver the baby but I had to make the money. Here I was nine months pregnant working while he was out "chilling" with some of his friends.

While we were talking, I happened to hear some heels trotting against my wood floor on the other end of the phone. I don't hesitate to say what's on my mind, especially when it came to my home. I asked him was there someone in my home, or was he walking around the house in heels being sarcastic. He of course got upset and hung up the phone. There was no reason why at nine months pregnant I should be dealing with that type of nonsense. But I was. I was enraged and wanted to get to the bottom of this. That night I became the pregnant detective. I called my supervisor and told them I had to leave. I probably said I was having contractions. Working in a predominately male environment, they wanted me to get the hell out of the jail before my water broke. It was three in the morning and I'm driving like a bat out of hell from Northampton to Springfield. I pulled in our gated apartment building directly outside of our building. I went to check on whether or not he was in the house...he was gone. I was furious and knew that nobody had business out at 3:30 or 4:00 in the morning. I was adamant on catching him so I decided to camp out in my SUV to see when he got home. I went in the house got some snacks and watched all the activity outside of our apartment that night. Every car that slowed down my heart began to race. I wanted to know who she was and why? How could he still be playing games after we lost our first child? Why the hell am I sitting here in this car pregnant and waiting, what could I do if I catch him?

6 am rolls around and my energy level is depleted. I ran out of snacks and my body was exhausted. Very few cars came down the street and I started to lose hope in catching him. 6:59 am in between me falling in and out of consciousness I see a minivan coming down the hill slowly. I didn't expect for him to get out of a car like that but sure enough, 7:00 am he and Tasha (the name was changed specifically for this story) stop right at the front of our apartment

gates. I see them in the van share some hug or a kiss and he notices my car parked outside the gate. I guess they caught a glimpse of me and sped off. I was furious. Tasha was actually a friend of my close friend, which I actually found disturbing. I knew they talked every once in a while, but I never thought in that manner. I drove to a friend's house crying telling them the secrets, I the detective had unveiled. I was determined to go back home and get some sleep. I wanted to know what the hell he could possibly say, since I caught him with my own two eyes. I turned the key to the house exhausted and still dressed in my correctional officer uniform, to find him standing looking pathetic in the nursery room. I could never forget the expression of guilt on his face. I was tired and fed up. This time though... I looked him in the face and I said nothing.

He was lost. No yelling or screaming at the top of my lungs. Our Indian neighbors below us were well aware of our toxic relationship. They were united in love by family making the choice for them; we on the other freely chose each other and lacked the level of commitment. This was when I began to believe that love is not enough. I found out what he didn't want me to know, another romance outside of our relationship. This time he didn't deserve my words, not a breath or sound of anguish. I was pissed and I found what I was looking for ...now what the hell was I going to do with this information? Seek and you shall find on a late night lookout.

PROMISES...

He promised to never hurt you again, but the only problem is he forgot to make that promise to himself...

What he can't do for self...he can't do for you.

BLAME GAME...

Everyone has played this game at some point in their life with a loved one. It is an unfair game that consists of insecure players. Players that are aware of the moves they made, but not how it affects the emotions of their loved ones. I believe they are aware, just at the time their selfishness kicks in. Their need to win or be right, trumps their loved ones emotional state. We have all played this game, and even blamed others for our own decisions. It is easier to point the finger at someone else, than to hold yourself accountable. Understanding the part you play in the game, and the results of the relationship, is beneficial to your personal growth. Everyone has been talking about cheating in all of our popular television shows and media. This day and age, cheating and infidelity has become so easy due to technological advances. The dating apps that are specifically for hookups, and direct messaging, allow for emotional connections to be made via technology. Those emotional connections then lead to physical meet ups and eventually trust broken between a committed relationship. Once caught, there are those players that find themselves easing their conscious by blaming their partner. When it comes to infidelity, the only person to blame is the one who acted out the behavior/action. It is important for the person being blamed, not to own this. When a person goes outside of the relationship, and makes the decision to break their commitment, they should only blame self. Even if there are issues within the committed relationship, communication should have occurred stating the issues within the relationship. The player should have also evaluated the pros and cons of their decision prior to acting on an immediate desire. Blaming someone else for your shortcomings denies you of the valuable lesson of self-discipline. Instead of confronting the player's issue, they rather pass on the bucket to the loved one. A bucket filled with all of the players personal issues for their loved one to carry.

Outside of infidelity, there is the blaming for your current situation. The player blames their parents, family, job, or just about anything for their current circumstances. The cards you were dealt with all are a result of decisions you have made in the past. When confronted with them, it's easier to pass on to others, as opposed to face the underlying issue...you! Blaming others is a lack of self-love. It is avoidance at its best. Until you stop blaming others for your lack of success, will you realize you hold the key to your future. Children result to the blame game in fear of being disciplined by an adult. Adults result to the blame game in fear of facing their underlying issues. It's a temporary fix for a long-term problem, and until confronted, the cycle of blame will repeat itself. The person will continue to encounter the same situations with different people, and the same results. Until they realize they are responsible, they will remain stagnant. The player of the blame game will always lose in the end.

CLOUDY MIRRORS...

For some of us, the way we see ourselves is not truly who we are. In fact the ego really creates this facade of greatness and lack of shortcomings. A true person on the path to self-discovery has endured the emotional rollercoaster of seeing through a clear mirror. Everyone that we attract is a reflection of who we are or what we are at that very moment. The very things that are highlighted to you through the negative behaviors of another, is you finally seeing through a clear mirror. Everything vibrates on a frequency, what our mind thinks we attract. Trust me it's a hard pill to swallow but every circumstance and situation we unconsciously attract it. Your baby daddy that you really dislike or girlfriend that betrayed you is all a reflection of your internal thoughts. Wiping the mirror clean takes a lot of self-reflection and pain because of the truth being revealed. That very thing that you dislike about someone, and you continuously encounter is a lesson for you to learn. I had to learn the hard way, about the things I don't want, to become clear with the things I do want. My emotions have always been valid, and the answers have always been internal. I have sought out answers through books, loved ones, and others through experiences, only to realize every situation and circumstance is tailored to you. Just you! The truth hurts. The best advice I can give is to spend time evaluating those who frustrate you, because deep down they are a reflection of you and the reason for your cloudy mirror. Getting an understanding of them clears your mirror of the debris. So you can make the appropriate changes of thought to create a different life for yourself. A life without doubt and support of the ego. Stop looking at yourself through that cloudy mirror.

MIRROR...

All it takes is one person to expand your perspective of self, life, places or things. This will show you what you are truly worth. We engage in destructive behaviors, and inflict our pain unto others from our negative view of self. When someone hurts you, don't mirror to them their pain and brokenness, by reacting to their negativity. Mirror to them their underlying beauty and wholeness. You just may be the gift that soul needs.

IF I ONLY KNEW...

I swear I have gained so much more respect and understanding for her as a parent. I guess it's normal as humans to point out what others have lacked, especially as a teenager or a young adult. I recall having conversations with my mother about certain things that she used to do. Things that I would not approve of or things I believed she could have done more of. The problem with that is a lot of times we are a product of a vicious cycle. As much as we don't want to admit it we do take many of our parent's traits with us. Of course, it is natural to want to go a step beyond what our parents taught us when it comes to us parenting. I am sure we have all said well I won't do this or I won't do that and possibly catch ourselves mocking the same trait or habits of our parents. I remember calling my mother when I was pregnant with London. It was one of those days where I wasn't feeling like myself. Between working eleven to seven shift and constantly arguing with his father I felt terrible. I mean it is already bad enough that we as women have to endure so much to prepare for the baby. I think I was in my second trimester so everything was just huge. My feet were swelling and it was about the middle of summer or at least the beginning. My face was full of acne and my nose was spreading across my face. That was something my mom would say. I was excited because this was something that I always wanted especially for my spouse and I, but the timing and situation couldn't be any more difficult.

I mean here we were living in a house that I decided to try and rent to own alongside my father. We agreed he would help me by staying there with my younger brother for a year while his wife remained in Texas taking care of her mother. Once again I was rushing into something (meaning the house), that at that point in time was just not for me. Being a Taurus and very stubborn, I tend to try to make things work no matter how much time and effort it takes. I could imagine myself in Kindergarten trying to stick a square block in to a circle puzzle piece. That's really what it was. For a while, being the nice daughter that I was. I was trying to make things as comfortable for my father as possible. I knew things for him the past year were difficult, especially being a single parent to two teenage boys. One who was incarcerated at the time. I tried everything in my power to mask my father from his reality. I did everything I possibly could do to help out. Majority of the time I just wanted to make him smile. Here we go again people pleaser. For a while I made my room down stairs in the old colonial house that had two bedrooms and a garage. The house definitely was a fixer upper and I just thought of it as an opportunity for ownership.

Once again here I was adding to the list of projects. Little did I know! I spent the first couple of trimesters having the basement as my room. That day while on the phone with my mother I was upstairs in the freshly painted room. I figured at that point we were getting ready for the baby and I wanted everything to be perfect. The room was small and the rug semi new but that fresh coat of dark blue paint my spouse painted made it look a bit more modern. With my 32 inch TV and the AC, that is where I spent most of my days. Most likely that day he was out and about with one of his friends doing who knows what. I was upset and frustrated at everything most of the time but that day I was scared. I remember crying to my mother telling her my fear of being a failure as a parent. Her responding that there is no true way or manuscript on how to be a parent. I just couldn't understand myself a lot throughout my pregnancy. Something that I prayed for, cried about, and asked for, why was I still not happy. My spouse and I have had relationship issues for a while; prior to getting pregnant with London but having a baby together was what we both always talked about. How we envisioned the situation, I am sure was a bit different. Call it crazy but I recall wondering if my son was going to love me for me. I wanted it all. I worried about if we were going to have enough clothes, money, diapers, childcare, toys, even things like what my baby is going to look like. I pictured things to be so much more different. My picture was not reality. Although my picture was not my reality, my reality was my life. Here I was laying in this bed worrying about where he was, if I was going to be a good mother while on the phone with my mother yelling at me for thinking about things not your typical person would think about. Some people probably wouldn't even care. They just try their best. Me on the other hand I did not want to leave any room for mistakes. Just like the old me planning and trying to set certain time restraints. I wanted to do things the right way. Although I started off on a bad foot I was going to correct this. This was my mindset for the majority of my pregnancy. Seventy five percent of it was spent thinking, worrying, and stressing about things that I could not control. The other twenty five percent of it was trying to make that connection with London. Sitting here writing this I begin to tear up, because all the time that I wasted on other foolishness, I could have spent bonding with him. ***Only If I knew…***

RIGHT IN FRONT OF YOUR FACE...

When something goes missing, and we are on the frequency of lack, we go overdrive into panic mode. We do ourselves an injustice because our vision becomes blurred. We are unable to focus to attract the very thing we are looking for, or missing. It is when we slow down, control our vibrations, and become aware, will we be able to see exactly what we were looking for all along. This is what happened to me. I spent 32 years in panic mode, searching for what was always right in front of my face. Searching for what was always within me.

AMOUR LONDON

PSALM 51

Have mercy upon me, O God, according to thy lovingkindness: according unto the multitude of thy tender mercies blot out my transgressions. Wash me thoroughly from mine iniquity, and cleanse me from my sin. For I acknowledge my transgressions: and my sin is ever before me. Against thee, thee only, have I sinned, and done this evil in thy sight: that thou mightiest be justified when thou speakest, and be clear when thou judgest. Behold, I was shapen in iniquity; and in sin did my mother conceive me. Behold, thou desirest truth in the inward parts: and in the hidden part thou shalt make me to know wisdom. Purge me with hyssop, and I shall be clean: wash me, and I shall be whiter than snow. Make me to hear joy and gladness; that the bones which thou hast broken may rejoice. Hide thy face from my sins, and blot out all mine iniquities. Create in me a clean heart, O God; and renew a right spirit within me. Cast me not away from thy presence; and take not thy holy spirit from me. Restore unto me the joy of thy salvation; and uphold me with thy free spirit. Then will I teach transgressors thy ways; and sinners shall be converted unto thee. Deliver me from blood guiltiness, O God, thou God of my salvation: and my tongue shall sing aloud of thy righteousness. O Lord, open thou my lips; and my mouth shall shew forth thy praise. For thou desirest not sacrifice; else would I give it: thou delightest not in burnt offering. The sacrifices of God are a broken spirit: a broken and a contrite heart, O God, thou wilt not despise. Do good in thy good pleasure unto Zion: build thou the walls of Jerusalem. Then shalt thou be pleased with the sacrifices of righteousness, with burnt offering and whole burnt offering: then shall they offer bullocks upon thine altar.

MY LETTER TO LONDON…

London Kyrie,

Sometimes I sit back and wonder, if I was given one wish from God in reference to my time with you what would I ask for? The day you were brought into this world was bittersweet. I couldn't wait to hold you but the pain of waiting for you just to show sign of life, left me in a numb space. How selfish of me at many times in my life, wish to take my own life. For you not even have a chance at one. I knew you were gone the day I called the doctors. There I stood in front of my bathroom mirror naked, staring at my lifeless womb. I felt empty. For days you fought to live, in an environment that was created in sin. Your father and I loved each other but did not love ourselves. I remember seeing the ultrasound at a thirteen week appointment, praying you were a boy because you had your father's feet. I prayed to you every night just to remind you that not a day passes I don't think of you. I can feel your energy and spirit around me especially when I hear our song. I remember I used to sing Beyoncé "love on top" at the top of my lungs while dancing and rubbing my belly. I prayed for you. I prepared and was ready for that very moment. You made me realize that we are never truly prepared. I named you London because it was your father's nickname from his friends. To be honest I have no clue why besides his Haitian accent which has no ties to Europe. Kyrie came from the high school athlete that was being drafted in the NBA. Plus we have a family full of the letter K. You were supposed to be our gift. Your love was to mask the grief of us losing Gram; instead you passed exactly a year later. I wished there was something I could have done. I felt like I left you to fight a battle alone. I should have gone to another hospital to get a second opinion. With every year passing I just remember the experience as a bad nightmare. When I was told I had to give birth to you, I was enraged. I had to undergo birth and labor pains to deliver my son who was already gone. It was not fair!

I had to celebrate your existence and plan a funeral at the same time. Your father was so heart-broken but knew I wanted a Christmas tree. As we left the hospital after hearing the news, we rode in the car in complete silence. He decided to go out and get a live tree and decorate it. That night after everyone left, we laid together in our bed cuddling with you in my womb resting peacefully. I was so afraid of what to expect, my fear was I would not connect with you. You were truly an angel! You had a few bumps and bruises but you were a healthy baby boy. I was overdue so you were weighing in at almost 8 pounds just like your brother. There were so many people that were ready to love you but cried at the sight of you. You were a dream and a innocent life that had been taken too soon. I envied the women in hospital rooms next to me with the crying babies. I was special that day. I was the woman that lost her baby. I left the hospital empty handed with stretch marks, a stitched vagina, and breast preparing for milk....with no baby. Three months later I found out I was pregnant with your little brother Micah! I initially felt guilty. I constantly reminded you that no child would ever replace you and he didn't. I thought that once I had Micah that the bad memories would fade away. They didn't. I was anxious, and was asked by physicians to take anti-depressants during my pregnancy. I gave the doctors hell and worried about every little move he made. You were born vaginally and Micah C section. Mommy got best of both worlds. When Micah was born I called him you. Everyone mixed up the poor child's name. Every Birthday he has and every night we go to bed we pray for you. I am embarrassed at the way your father and I had turned out but grief and the loss of a child can make strange things happen. I wanted to know what your personality would be like or what would be your favorite food? Would Micah even be here if you would have lived? It has been almost six years and every 5th of December the nightmare begins. It brings about old emotions and pain from the grief we felt from losing you. So if I was to have just one opportunity to embrace you let it be in my dreams. My dream of you is you being embraced with the love of God and your grandmother Ruth. The whole time I was pregnant I was so upset that she wasn't there to experience this chapter in my life. I know she is looking after you like she does me. Spiritually whatever was going on you decided that life just wasn't for you yet. Just remember like I tell your brother I love you beyond the universe and the heavens. A mother's love is undying and strong. I will and have never forgotten you, as everything I do is for you and your brother. One day we will meet again. Until then, Rest in Peace London. Your footprints will forever be in my heart.

LONDON KYRIE EXANTUS 12/5/2011...

Thanksgiving 2010 was the last day that I saw my Grandmother. She was going back and forth to the hospital for pneumonia, but this stay was different. She was diagnosed with Lung Cancer and landed a lengthy stay in the hospital. Two weeks had passed before I made it my priority to go and visit. I spent most of my Thanksgivings as a young girl in her home. Things changed when we encountered death of my grandfather, aunt and uncle. Something about my grandmother died with them. I felt guilt going to her empty-handed, but hoped she was still happy about the fuchsia roses I bought her the last time. She bragged to all the nurses and doctors about how beautiful they were. It meant a lot to me because she loved flowers. I would do anything to put a smile on her face after being faced with death. When the doctors told her the diagnoses, I was there. She denied and cursed the doctors for even telling her something like that. She didn't understand Cancer, but her nicotine dependency throughout her life seemed to finally cause her body lethal damage. One in which she could not erase. In her mind the doctors weren't telling the truth, that was her story and she was sticking to it.

Thanksgiving day, I did not cook the Okra. That's all she wanted from me, nothing more nothing less. She loved my cooking and knew I could cook it, but Lard was never used in my kitchen. She told me how she wanted it but my schedule didn't permit me to even eat during this time. While I went to visit my grandmother, I was also visiting county jail, and working two jobs to maintain my household and a jail cell. I had lost about thirty pounds from working 24hrs straight some days, so my grandmother immediately took notice. "Girl you starting to look like that girl off the Jenny Craig commercial!" I could do nothing but laugh and reply "Jennifer Hudson". That day was different when I went to see her. She was at peace. Peace with the hospital food, peace that I came empty-handed, and peace with her illness. My grandmother gave the hospital workers hell most of the time, but Thanksgiving Day 2010, she was giving God thanks for her life. The visit was quiet as she sat and told me about who came to see her, "Where is that boyfriend of yours?" she asked. I had lied to her every visit by telling her he was at work. I was embarrassed and was not ready to hear what she had to say. When I decided to leave, I gave her a kiss on the cheek. That was the first time in twenty something years of my life was I able to be affectionate with this woman. With that kiss, she said nothing. She did not reject it, or tell me "get out of here with that mess." She accepted my kiss at peace. I left. Later that evening my grandmother went into cardiac arrest.

Thanksgiving Day 2011 my water broke.

Exactly a year later my son was born stillborn. I was asked by the doctors, if I wanted to see and hold him. Everything about that day was not normal. I did not know what to feel. I wanted to protect my son's father, because he was weak. His weakness had a lot to do with his guilt for the way he treated me during my pregnancy. I was giving birth and planning for death at the same time. I was afraid of what my child was going to look like because there was no amniotic fluid. I had to give birth to my son via vaginal with no natural fluids. My son had fought for days; here it was a week since thanksgiving. No one was able to realize that something was wrong. I trusted the doctors over myself, and I knew my body. The doctors gave me morphine and an epidural to numb my experience. My body swelled from the fluids. The amount of tears shed in that room, that day, could have replenished the womb that once carried my son. Fear does not live here anymore. I have endured pain and have seen many things no one should ever be exposed to. All I am left with is his footprints. There is life after loss.

WHEN DEATH HITS HOME...

When death hits home, it affects all those around us. We as humans tend to think of ourselves within such a small scale, that we don't realize how our behaviors, thoughts, and actions affect all those around us. I have to remind people all the time that death is not just the physical. Grieving or the five stages of grief do not just occur with the physical loss of a loved one. Grieving occurs within the process of letting go, dreams that we allowed to die, the death of a relationship or ones identity. Our relationship had died long before the death of our son. In fact, we both died in the process of forcing things to work with the very little tools we were given. My ex-husband was a man that was raised in an impoverished country, where many times he had no idea where his next meal would come from. I was spoiled by my single mother who thought materialistic things showed her emotional love or connection for me as her child. We were complete opposites. I'm a firm believer that the very things we did not have as a child we crave for as an adult. His focus was money, stability and loyalty. I desired love. I now understand that we all have different love languages, and express our love in differing ways. How you may want someone to show you they love you just may not be the way they were taught to love or know how.

We fought so much in our marriage because we were both angry over the lives we sacrificed. I recall my son's father telling me how different his life would have been if his mother raised him. He would have never been in trouble with the law, nor would he have behaved the way he did as a teen. Or would he? We all have a choice and when we choose to live life to others expectations and do things because we are "supposed" to, we slowly murder our own souls, committing spiritual suicide every time. We had the struggle love. The one in which we had no clue who we were but carried each other's burdens. A young couple, especially a young black couple can have a hard time trying to survive. There is no room for experiencing the positive side of the relationship when the two are surrounded by turmoil and society tearing them apart. Let alone the families that inflict their traditional dysfunction unto the new couple, setting them up for failure.

The night at the hospital when I called because of the lack of movement, I already knew something wasn't right. After the nurse came in to check the baby's heartbeat, her smile turned into an immediate sense of panic, I told my son's father to leave. For some strange reason I felt the need to protect him from the news we were about to receive. He didn't want to leave but I just needed time to digest all that was going on around me. When you experience this level of trauma the time seems to move so fast. Within a split second your life can change forever. All my life I struggled to be the person that everyone wanted me to be. That day, I not only felt like I failed him, but I also failed myself. All the technology and medical advancements in this world and women are still losing their children. I just couldn't understand after carrying a child for 41 weeks, I was beyond the finish line, only to hear that I would be crossing this finish line alone. I physically became a woman, my body carried life for nine months and the only proof I had left were the stretch marks, a box of his belongings, and a set of footprints. I fell to my knees in tears as I was asked to make my first phone call. My son's father was outside of the door making phone calls to family and loved ones. I don't recall much but remember my best friend at the time running through the door with her foot in a cast, she was someone who has known me for many years and has seen my struggles. My eyes are filling with tears writing this as I can visualize her face. I still to this day don't know how she got to the hospital so fast. She came to save me, but it was too late. I was physically there but spiritually I was gone. In the black family, or maybe it was just my grandmother's southern myth, when a person dies a child is born. My grandmother went into cardiac arrest and died around the same time the year prior. I just knew that London would be the new birth of the family, a blessing after the grief. There is no way a woman can go back to being the person she was after losing a child. I saw my grandmother lose two of her children and her husband in the same year. Like the bible story of Naomi and Ruth. My grandmother and I finally had something we shared. We not only shared the same DNA but also her pain now ran through my veins. I thought my son was the one to be born but instead it was the rebirth of me.

TRUST...

Trust begins with self. Self-esteem, self-confidence, and self-awareness are the building blocks to trust. Once you have conquered these within yourself, the trust you have built within will be projected on the relationships you build on the outside. Trust begins with self because we have a choice. The problem is that with certain relationships, people don't believe or understand they actually do have a choice. One thing that seems common in situations with women's health and fetal loss is the trust factor. In healthcare, trust is extremely important when seeking a physician. You trust that they will provide you with confidentiality and the best possible treatment. A lot of times, patients place an extensive level of trust into healthcare providers, to the point where they lose their inner voice. A physician only understands you, through you. You're diagnosed by the symptoms that are visible, and by the symptoms you have communicated to the physician you have personally experienced. Self-awareness is important in this case because we as women should be mindful and aware of how our body works. We need to monitor intake and output, menstrual cycles, and also important our emotional state. Pay attention to what works for your skin and how your body reacts. You should be aware of what is not "normal" to you. During my 5k run for stillbirth awareness, there were signs with short facts about stillbirth. One that stood out to me was that 90% of women knew something was not right. That is a high percentage. Many women including myself, experiencing childbirth and pregnancy the first time place extensive levels of trust in physicians. I'm sure you have seen the movies where the woman gets extremely upset because her normal doctor is sick or unavailable. She wants someone who knows her medical history and one that she trust.

The issue lies when an individual's degree and certificates, clouds your judgement or trust within yourself. I don't care how long someone has been in practice, every patient is different. Situations may be similar, but all patients are different. Many women, especially first time mothers, place that extensive level of trust in physicians. Trust in which sometimes clouds their own judgment about their own needs and desires. Treatment options, birthing options, and self-care are all things very rarely discussed or talked about. Doctors today have a bunch of patients, so remembering everyone and who wants what can be difficult. So as patients, it is important to ask questions. If you don't feel like something is right, ask for more testing or resources for answers. As women our voices are silenced through ego because of the fear that one is more intelligent than the other. Any individual with a higher level of education understands that there is always an opportunity to learn something new. Its unfortunate when I had encountered this situation, I did not push to understand the information that was provided to me. I just stood by their word in my trust, at that time. This does not just apply to fetal loss but also anxiety and depression. I hate to say this but hospitals and doctors' offices have become primarily business. More focused on the financial gains as opposed to the well-being and options for the best treatment for their patients.

Anti-depressant medications amongst women are being handed out like candy on Halloween. Women or patients are not being provided with alternative options. Anyone that has ever tried a diet pill knows it requires some level of work from you. You may need to change you eating habits, exercise, or lifestyle to enhance to ability of the pill to work for you. Same goes for other medications. Our bodies are our internal compass; they alert us when something is wrong. Trust yourself enough to challenge your physician, and have a health plan or goal for yourself. When pregnant ask questions, and create a birthing plan you see fit for you. Don't silence yourself or health needs, due to the intimidation of one's degree. The more trust you have within yourself, the better choices you will make about your life and the life you carry. Asking questions, raising awareness, and expressing concerns can save a life. It may be your first time, but it is the physicians first time working with you.

THERE IS POWER IN LETTING GO...

There is so much power in letting go! It took me a while to recognize it, but I felt the need to share my story. People have no idea how I conceived Micah. I mean beyond the sexual activity that I had to partake in. I mean on a spiritual level, his conception was divine timing. I always get a laugh from my friends when I tell them he is the easy bake oven baby. He was made on a rooftop of a hospital in less than four minutes. His father and I decided to do things the right way this time. We became so close after the loss of our first son that we decided to get married. The closeness wasn't healthy. In fact I clung to him for the fear of losing him as well. Within two years I had lost both, my grandmother, my newborn son and the thought of losing him made my emotional grip even tighter. Micah was the gift that we received as a result of me *letting go* of all my fears. As most mothers do, I spent months preparing for London right up until my due date. I spent time preparing his nursery and shopping for all his needs. I even got a new apartment, and cleared out the negative energy of some family and friends. I did what I thought I was supposed to do in preparation of my new title as a mother. When he passed, I spent days in my apartment, with visitors coming in and out to check on our wellbeing. I became so comfortable with all of the company that when alone, I became afraid of darkness. My husband at the time did his best to make sure I was never alone, and one day while at work, I did the unthinkable.

I called my best friend at the time, to tell her to bring her cousin by to take everything out of the nursery. At the time her cousin was about five or six months, and was the only other person I knew expecting. I really wanted to give everything to a person that greatly appreciated it, and she was the first person that came to mind. I just wanted it all out of my house. I got sick of physically looking at my dreams shattered but nicely arranged like a museum display of what life was supposed to be. My girlfriend at the time thought I was losing it. She asked me multiple times if this was something that I wanted to do. One thing about me is that when my mind is finally made up, that is it. There is no turning back for me. One thing I regret is not talking to my then husband about it at the time. Then again, if I did, he probably would have talked me out of it. I watched as they removed everything from my home piece by piece. To be honest once everything was gone I don't recall shedding a tear. My husband and I got into a huge argument that evening when he got home. He wanted to hold on, and I was ready to let go! People said not to get rid of it because you will have another child. Or, "put it in storage so you don't have to prepare when the next child comes. Why would you do that?" The answer is for my sanity. I slowly, opened up to holding other babies, and celebrating the life of other couples and their newborns. I still hurt from the loss of my son, but I no longer wanted to be stuck on the events of Dec 2011.

Three months later, I ran into my best friend's mother while leaving an attorney's office. She proceeds to tell me that my best friends were expecting at the time. I sat in my car for at least an hour crying **crocodile tears.** My husband and I at the time were grieving in our separate ways. Him though partying and bullshit, me through facing my demons head on.

In our physical bodies, we are more inclined to physically or mentally hold on to things. The power in letting go is letting God or the Universe know you have faith. We continuously try to play in these roles, trying to control every aspect of our lives, only to find much of this life we have no control over. The power of letting is knowing that there is something more for you. Letting go is allowing space for the new. When we hold on through trying to control, we lose or power, only to allow the situation to end up controlling us. When we let go and surrender the power of trying to control, and allow what is for us to be received by us, life becomes much simpler. What is meant for you will always be, and nothing that is for you can be taken or compromised by anyone but you. There is so much good in change and miracles that occur when you realize the power of letting go. Holding on through action is backed by fear. Letting go and doing so with love, only life changing situations can occur. When we hold on to events, people, and circumstances we are stunting our evolution. Forcing what we thought was meant to be, as opposed to what is to be. I have learned that no matter what the circumstance is I will let it go, always realizing that whatever the outcome, I will be okay! Letting go is my silent physical prayer to God or the Universe, letting them know that I trust them even when I can't see what they are constructing behind the scenes. *Let Go!*

CROCODILE TEARS...

Today I cried! No I didn't shed a tear, I shed crocodile tears. I knew this day would come but I had absolutely no idea. It has been exactly three months and eight days since I lost my son. I personally believe I had been doing so well dealing. I was still functioning but did not realize the real damage this situation has done to both my heart and my soul. Although I had not started any form of therapy yet, I have been writing and my creative juices have been flowing. I have been to a few services at a local church and went to a support group once. Since the day that I had found out that my son has passed, I had not had an emotional breakdown. Trust me I was concerned because I had thought to myself that this can't be right. I must have some issues or something seeing as how I managed to continue functioning regularly. I thought that I had coped with the situation a little better because of my past experiences with a lot of deaths in my family. I don't know if I was trying to show my strengths to everyone or trying to prove myself. I know one of the reasons was I was more concerned for how my husband felt rather than dealing with my own feelings first. I have not been alone since London's death. As strange as it may seem, I also had this sudden fear of darkness. During the night, I recall myself having this sudden panic attack because of the darkness and being alone. I don't know what it was but I began to associate darkness with death. I recall my chest tightening and me forcing myself to fall asleep so that I could wake up to a new day with light. It was so bad that I even became fearful of previews of the new scary movies that were coming out. How I associated my traumatic experience with scary movies I have no clue. I just wanted nothing to do with death. My husband was by my side the whole time in the hospital. So once we left I did not want him to leave my side. Honestly I enjoyed the fact that we had his mother stay with us for a week to basically help around the house. I needed others to be around because at this point solitude was my worst nightmare. I believe my husband had sensed this onset fear of mine and quickly adjusted to the role as my constant companion. He felt obligated to try to be around me as much as possible. With his mother present she made sure that we ate, the house was clean, and that I tended to my daily needs. My husband and I sat back dreading the day that she would leave to go back to Pennsylvania to her own family. We would have to face our nightmare and reality together alone.

Our relationship prior to losing our son had faced my different trials and tribulations but this wasn't just the icing on the cake this was the surprise birthday party! We have endured many things but this was yet another challenge that we had to face. This was only the beginning. It was March and my husband had decided to take a trip for his birthday. If he could he would probably celebrate the whole entire month. Hey he was young and enjoyed hanging out with his friends. He asked if we could take a trip to *Miami* to visit some of his family and friends. Of course I was back at work and my time would not permit for me to go unless I called out sick for those few days. At first I was excited because I had never been to Miami and would love to meet his other family members, but I was just returning to work and had used all of my accrued vacation and sick time. What would I look like calling out after just returning from maternity leave? My husband did not want to hear it. Now that I look back I wish I had gone. I wish I would have called out. Every woman I had spoken to about my husband being down there looked at me as if I had five heads. "You let your husband go down to Miami alone on Spring Break?" I originally thought nothing of it. I even went as far as to rent a vehicle for him and a friend to drive down. I felt confident that work was where I needed to be and he would behave himself and respect his family he would be leaving here in Springfield. So I told him to go ahead. I initially was fine with the idea but afterwards my feelings had changed. Now that I think about it I was so concerned with me agreeing to this break away. We both needed a stress reliever but at that point someone had to work to pay the bills and that person had to be me.

As I think back now we both needed a vacation. I rushed back to work back to my life style as if nothing ever happened. He decided to grieve differently and party his pain away, never once speaking his name or stating how he felt. So with my spouse in Miami for the week, this meant for me to learn how to face being all alone again. So what drove me to crocodile tears? The first day after my husband had left for Miami, I had run in to a good friend of mine's mother. This actually is one of the amazing women responsible for my strength and success today. This woman has known me since a pre-teen and helped shaped me in to the hard-working woman who I am today. She had met me for a meeting in which she was excited as usual to see me and the fact that I was doing well. We had seen each other a few times since I had given birth to London in which she was in the labor room holding one of my legs. She had experienced this traumatic event alongside me and since was concerned of my well-being. Her daughter was also a close friend of mine and at this point in time had disconnected herself and her spouse from spending time with my husband and I. Things were rough between us and many people felt like they were in between making it difficult to maintain friendships. Honestly I don't think they understood or will ever understand the toll just losing a child has on a relationship. Her mother had asked if we had spoken to each other. I believe at some point I had tried to reach out but received no response. I was told by her mother weeks ago that my friend had found an apartment with her spouse and that they had moved in together. I was extremely excited because that was a big transition for the two and it showed they were becoming even more serious as a couple. We would all hang out together in the past. My spouse and I being a more seasoned couple had lived together for a while. I had introduced this couple to each other about three years ago and they have been together ever since. The thing that I was about to hear I could not believe. It wasn't the fact as if I did not know that it was going to happen. The fact that her mother told me had bothered me the most. I felt as though someone had punched me in my chest and knocked the wind out of me. "You know she is pregnant?" Her mother stated. No of course not. I have not spoken to her. I wanted all but not to feel the way that I was feeling. I wanted to celebrate and be a part of their new beginning. London's death and my experience would not allow me to. I used every ounce of energy to spare myself the embarrassment of crying on a Main St. I just got off of work and was extremely exhausted and now had to listen to news like this.

First Beyonce, and now her. I believe her mother had begun to notice the effects of the news she had just reported to me. She even began to give me that way too familiar head tilt and slight frown. The universal sign of sympathy or so it had become to me. I even recall all the medical care professionals that I worked with during the course of this event displaying the same face. I was not upset at the fact that they were expecting. I was upset that they did not tell me. I just knew I had to find a way to cut myself from that situation and soon. My emotions exploded once alone. My mind began to run a thousand miles per hour. I thought about everything. I replayed my traumatic scene. My body was so tense from my bruised heart and mind of **envy**. I just knew that they would go on and have a happy ending. Why the fuck did something like this happen to me? Why would God do something like this to me? Do they not want to be around me because I am cursed? Are they afraid the same thing was going to happen to them? I came to realization that this couple had endured this experience with us and have seen me at my worst. All I could think of that moment was I wanted to be held. My husband was in Miami, My mother miles away, my father and I weren't speaking so I had to face being alone. I had to face being alone and reliving my tragedy over and over again. One thing I learned from that day in particular was importance of support consistently down the road. I had a great amount of support including my family whom I had kept my distance, show a great amount of support when they received that phone call.

The thing is most people don't know what to say. This is something that is not supposed to happen. Everyone prepares you for the stressors that come along with becoming a new parent. No one speaks about the potential what ifs. It is such a worldly sensitive subject that you seldom hear about. I might have heard about stillbirth twice during my pregnancy and did not even attempt to read the chapter "Complicated pregnancies" in the pregnancy bible "What to expect when you're expecting" until I had found out about my two vessel cord. There are no public service announcements, or conversations at prenatal visits regarding this issue that terribly happens often. Some women may disagree with what I may say but I feel most of these women would like to speak at some point in their lives about their loss. Please understand that your support is not just needed at that tragic time but also for a lifetime. No matter if your child was just conceived and lost through a miscarriage or later as a newborn. No one person can determine your relationship with that child. Since my son's death I have been to the mall (Baby heaven), spent time with an infant that is the same age my son would have been. It has been so hard on my husband and I, to encounter people who had seen me pregnant and for them to ask how the baby is doing and the face I get is priceless after hearing my response. Or the look that I get now when they see Micah and try to do the math in there head. It is a look that no one could ever forget. A look that constantly reminds me how something like this is just not supposed to happen? But it did and it happened to me!

I would have given anything to have sleepless nights because of my crying child. Or walking around looking crazy because he would not let me sleep or tend to myself. Instead I have to face my experience head on every day when I see people that had saw me during my pregnancy, or when I look at myself in the mirror naked seeing the stretch marks around my navel. The changes my body has gone through **physically and emotionally without my son London.**

I had no clue at the time but I was pregnant with my second child at the time. There was healing within the very tears I shed.

JUST A REMINDER...

All I needed was a reminder! I may have left the hospital empty-handed but my heart was filled. Although at the time it was filled with nothing but confusion and anger, there was still love. I recall walking around my room when everyone had left, listening to the woman next to me comfort her crying child. I walked out of the room to get some ice, because my room felt dark and empty. No one came in our room to clean or even ask how we were. The professionals that went to school for years, were at a loss for words for what occurred. I guess during your residency they don't discuss cases like mine. As I walked back towards my room, I recalled this symbol or card they placed on the door. It was of a leaf surrounded by a dark purple background holding a tear drop. After doing some research, the symbol is to represent intense loss and hope for the future. I still cringe every time I see this card hanging on the outside of someone's door. I just want to go in and hug them and remind them that everything will be okay, and that this day will forever mark your heart and change how you view life and things. The leaf separates you from all the other rooms.

I always considered myself different, but that day, I didn't want to be. I wanted what everyone else had! The balloons, excited family members, and a screaming crying newborn. My innocence was broken, a dream was shattered, and I was left with a room prepared for a baby. I thought I was ready; I had everything materialistically, and emotionally. I walked back into my room alone not realizing this was the part of the healing process. I have abandonment issues, so I was forced to be alone. Forced to reevaluate my life and see what changes I was required to make...all doing so in solitude. No one knew what to say and I just wanted to be reminded that through it all, I am London's mother!

If you don't know what to say to someone who has experienced some form of fetal loss just remind them...

Questions

Am I sure I am ready for this?

Too late to turn back now, this can't be God's wish.

Am I strong enough to deal with a situation like this?

Seems unbearable but underneath there is underlying strength.

Am I in a dream or is this a nightmare?

A bit of both, so count your blessing even though not many are there.

Have I done all that I could do?

To blame is not the answer, especially not on you.

What does this make me after all I had suffered?

You are not just a woman, you are also a mother.

EVERYTHING HAPPENS FOR A REASON...

It is interesting to me how the life I had in mind was not exactly the life that God had intended for me. I remember reading a quote about how the road that we try to avoid actually is the road that helps to determine who you are in the end. I attended a sermon at a local church a few weeks after London had passed away for the Christmas sermon. As usual we tried just about everything including Bingo, to keep ourselves busy. The sermon was based on the original Christmas story. I have not been to church in a while but I knew it was something that we needed. One thing I've noticed after losing a child was that my confidence was at an all-time low. I will admit I was never really an over-confident woman. I felt as though while in public places people could read my deep dark secret. People would look at me and say" oh, she is the one who lost her baby." That day I made sure I got dressed to make myself feel better to bring my self-esteem up a notch. I have had plenty of those days where I did not want to run in to someone I knew in my sweatpants .But imagine how it feels to run into someone when that person knew that you were pregnant and you have nothing to show for it.

The local church that we went to was packed as usual and we were running a little late. I always hated showing up late because it seemed as if all eyes were on your every move. My husband hated the fact that if you are late to the church you have to attend the service downstairs in which it's a much smaller room and the service is viewed on the TV screen. He of course would have rather attended another church... As we were headed for the door disappointed that we wouldn't be able to find a seat the sister of a close friend who is also the main singer at the church was amazed to see us. I know she knew of our situation and wanted us to be a part of the church that day. She was so adamant about us staying for service that she made us our own row by adding chairs to a back pew. I truly admire her efforts for trying to get us to hear the word that day. Especially after giving the ushers a dirty look as if to say you better not say anything to me. We were eventually moved by one of the older Ushers because we kept getting in the way. That day we were placed in the front. The closest we had ever been. My husband had always felt some type of way about this church saying you need to be VIP to get in, so I guess that day we had our passes. The pastor went on to talk about the birth of Jesus and how Mary and Joseph weren't actually in the best situation. They were refused places to stay or even for a room to give birth. A lot of people were against them. Joseph was not even the father and to top it off Jesus was born in the most unsanitary places ... a manger.

What the pastor was trying to point out was that if Mary had known the type of circumstances she would have been in she would have never signed up for it. Little did she know the gift that she was given was going to be worth all the trials and tribulations. If I would have known, I would have never signed up for this. Neither would the other women whom have suffered the loss of a child. Even though I knew it in my heart the worst thing at that time to say to me was "Everything happens for a reason." It is beyond true that "Everything does happen for a reason".

THIEF IN MY HOME…

What's done in the dark always rears its ugly head in the light. His words, in addition to his actions, were never trustworthy. He lied and stole from his family, but somehow I thought he would be different when it came to me. This time he robbed me of my identity and broke my spirit. I allowed him in. I gave him the key. I invited the burglar into my house, and tried to make it a home for him.

SCREAM...

His soul screamed. I never heard his cry for help. I was drowning as his cries were silenced within my darkness. It was as if we both were stuck in a maze, only to never find each other. When pain hits home, it is every man for self. They are drowning so how can you expect them to save you?

EMOTIONS DRIVE OUR PERSPECTIVE...

Just like trying to read a book in the dark...I struggled to understand your contents. I couldn't see you. It was until I created my own light, did clarity present itself. My internal light shined bright enough, so that I could finally see. I could finally read your story and revel in your chapters. In the dark, I couldn't understand you. Within the light, your story has meaning.

MEN IN BLACK...

I haven't seen this movie in a while but was always intrigued by the magical pen that erased memories. The best way to describe my experience when I left the hospital and months in the grieving process was this "magical memory eraser" pen. Losing a child is a touchy subject, one that makes people doubt their faith. Loss of a loved one never is easy, but the situations leading up to it and how it occurs makes one begin to question life and its purpose. How we lose someone can really prolong the healing process in my personal belief. Elisabeth Kubler Ross created the five stages of grieving to identify the emotional rollercoaster you ride through the healing process. Denial, Anger, bargaining, depression and acceptance are all things we may experience with any form of loss (not just in the physical). Oh by the way, they don't always happen in this particular order either. For me anger became my best friend along with negativity, hence the reason I eliminate myself from relationships. I felt misunderstood and no one knew what to say...so they said nothing. Men in black became a reality and the "magical memory eraser" affected everyone around me. No one remembered just a few months ago that I was nine months pregnant waddling around excited to meet my little one. Everyone failed to mention that my pregnancy existed. I was avoided like the plague and my relationship took on another set of bricks. No one spoke of the elephant in the room, and allowed me to live in my anger space.

I though getting married could save me, I thought he could save me, and I thought my friends could save me. I knew death very well, but any physician or healthcare worker will tell you, you will never get used to it. Like every birth story death has its unique approach. The closer the relationship you had with the individual, the more you evaluate your life and its purpose. Nothing matters when birth or death occurs. The only thing that matters at that point is the now. I yearned for someone to come out of the magical pens trance and just acknowledge my pain. I wanted to feel connected with the rest of the world but my innocence of society had been broken. While everyone lives like they have an eternal life and defined themselves by career, material things, and relationship statuses...I knew and know now that all these things meant nothing. One day a co-worker of mine came to me and said "you are the strongest woman, I know and I'm hurt this happened to you". I cried like a baby. Only if everyone knew that the simplest sign of affection and a hug could move that person to the next process of healing. The day of the funeral is not the only day to send your condolences, check in six months or a year from the date. The absence or loss of things can create an overpowering appreciation. You learn not to take things for granted. Be kind to people because you never know their story, because trust me they all have one. I feel as though I have experienced a sense of awakening through this traumatic experience. So while everyone was affected by the "magical memory eraser", I remained cool like Will Smith with my black shades on learning to face the demons head on. Open your eyes and heart to the positive and negatives in life. Death and life are the collateral beauty. We as humans focus more on what we don't have rather than what we do. Your loved one can never be replaced but just think of the many gifts they have left you.

SAY SOMETHING/SAY NOTHING...

People worry about what they can say to ease a loved one's pain...your presence is enough.

COPE VS. CONCEAL...

The doctor's explained to me the importance of going through the birthing process. London was born vaginally, Micah born via emergency C–section. I wanted to go through this process with the least pain experienced possible. I wanted to feel and see absolutely nothing. I am now grateful for the experience, because they taught me the importance of facing my fears. Going through the experience, instead of avoiding it began the healing process. It is important for you to feel everything. To feel my pain, and process it gave me a broader perspective of my circumstances. I was able to embrace the light and the darkness of death. In my family, we are not taught to cope, rather we are taught to conceal. Emotions are concealed through weed, alcohol, and other street drugs. Fuck whoever told me I was the weakest women they know. My crazy was defined as a woman consumed with sadness. I was angry, envious, and disappointed with everyone including GOD. I even tried to distract myself and the problems still arose. I had to face death head on like a car crash. I had no clue if I would make it out alive.

I'm still here.

APRES LONDON

PSALM 91...

He that dwelleth in the secret place of the most high shall abide under the shadow of the Almighty. I will say of the LORD, He is my refuge and my fortress: my God; in him will I trust. Surely he shall deliver thee from the snare of the fowler, and from the noisome pestilence. He shall cover thee with his feathers, and under his wings shalt thou trust: his truth shall be thy shield and buckler. Thou shalt not be afraid for the terror by night; nor for the arrow that flieth by day; Nor for the pestilence that walketh in darkness; nor for the destruction that wasteth at noonday. A thousand shall fall at thy side, and ten thousand at thy right hand; but it shall not come nigh thee. Only with thine eyes shalt thou behold and see the reward of the wicked. Because thou hast made the LORD, which is my refuge, even the most

High, thy habitation; there shall no evil befall thee, neither shall any plague come nigh thy dwelling. For he shall give his angels charge over thee, to keep thee in all thy ways. They shall bear thee up in their hands, lest thou dash thy foot against a stone. Thou shalt tread upon the lion and adder: the young lion and the dragon shalt thou trample under feet. Because he hath set his love upon me, therefore will I deliver him: I will set him on high, because he hath known my name. He shall call upon me, and I will answer him: I will be with him in trouble; I will deliver him, and honor him. With long life will I satisfy him and shew him my salvation.

LESSONS LEARNED...

You can either choose to go through the pain…by learning to control your emotions through discipline.

Or

You can be forced to go through the pain. This will result in time spent on healing.

The interesting thing about life is we get to choose how we learn in many cases…not all.

DECEMBER 24, 2011…

December 24, 2011, I said "I do". I made a commitment to love you, more than I loved myself. I wore a black dress over my swollen body. My breast filled with milk, and no child to feed. There was no ring, or a large wedding party. A small wedding party of four, in a two bedroom apartment. A few days before the wedding, we decided why not make it official. We have struggled in love for this long, why not continue. They say times can get hard in long term relationships, and since we held hands walking through hell, why not? We got married in front of the Christmas tree you just had to get, the day I came home from delivering London. In your heart you felt a sense of guilt for the way you treated me. We got married in front of the same two witnesses that seen the abuse. The same couple that watched the emotional and physical struggle of a toxic version of love witnessed the contractual agreement of two troubled souls.

I wanted confirmation for my abandonment issues. I just lost my son, and I thought I would die if I lost you. In reality, in that black dress, I was attending my funeral. The death of a woman, committing to a man who was incapable of loving her the way she deserved. We both weren't ready. We had no idea what we were doing. All we knew was we already had been playing house. We both wanted to do it the right way. We thought we were doing what was right. That day I threw away my dreams of being a Kleinfield bride. I accepted my fate, and I settled. He loved me, in his own sick and twisted way. I didn't love me, so why wouldn't I stay. I thought losing you too, would be the death of me. Christmas Eve, three weeks after giving birth to my stillborn son, whatever was left of me died. I was far from home. I was far from the woman I was meant to be.

TITLE DOES NOT GIVE VALUE...

I thought having the ring would fix my relationship with my ex. Like many women, I believed that things would miraculously change and for the better. Instead things got worse. As women, I think we are taught socially what a relationship is supposed to be like and what to expect. However, in all reality this is not the case for everyone. Not everyone wants the same thing. Movies and shows skip over the trials that it took for the relationship to flourish. We see the wedding and the women saying yes to the dress but what about life afterwards. I am a fan of "Say yes to the dress" and watch it daydreaming of the wedding I did not have. We didn't have the money for a huge wedding, let alone the friends or family to attend. My ceremony was in my apartment on Christmas Eve witnessed by two of our best friends, and we were happy! Or at least that is what I thought. It was something we said we wanted to do a long time ago, but were not prepared for such responsibility and commitment. We were both young and doing what we thought was right. I was his wife, so I immediately thought I would come first. That all the pain of our past would be gone and we would miraculously move on to a brighter future. All because of a piece of paper, ring, and vow. Wrong! Now, as I am getting older and wiser through experience, relationships should be valued by the love (GOD) and how one makes you feel. As a woman, we are taught the importance of being claimed, like a piece of property. A man can claim you and defend your honor, and turn right around and disrespect you through his behavior when you're not present.

When I started dating again, I might have scared a few guys off because of my first date statement. "Look, I am dating with the intentions of a relationship." Now that I think about it, I wasn't just setting expectations; I was blocking the experience before it happened. Now that I think of it, I sounded pretty desperate. I turned dating into a job, and didn't enjoy getting to know the person. I was exhausted from the past hurt and pain and wanted the "good man" now! We may think we know what we deserve but when we receive it are not emotional prepared. Don't get me wrong it's fine to set your goals for dating, but I realize that allowing things to flow will allow you to get to know each other without the pressure. I don't know why I acted in this manner but I felt like I was running out of time. I'm like the older I get, the harder he will be to find. Or, the longer that I remain single the more "independent/strong female" I will become (I was told men don't like that). Just like every other single woman out here, I wanted to be claimed. I wanted someone to parade me on their social media as the love of their life. I wanted a picture perfect relationship. Dammit I wanted the title! Now, as I look beyond the surface, I'm okay with coasting. There is no need to hurry love. I see to many women with the title left unhappy because they are slowly losing themselves to fit the title someone else gave them. I see women who waited years for the ring after breakups and heart-break and finally get it. They don't realize they are carrying the physical evidence of what could be as to what the relationship truly is. We grieve the things that could have been, and my heart breaks for the fact that they don't know. He can tell you who you are to him, but his actions convey his value of you to others. As women we compete for this title, for someone to call you their own. At this point in my life, I am all for the experiences. I want to fall into an unforced love that feels as natural as me taking a breath. I want loving me to come easy for him. I'm good with the title, been there done that... show me how you value me through your actions. I gave myself a title that I will uphold...the title of his queen productively waiting for her King.

MIAMI…

Three months of vacation time spent on trying to get my life back together. I hate America for expecting a woman to snap back after she just created life. The sad part is I had to use my vacation time, for the grieving and death of my son. No beach, sand, drinks in my hand, or a tan, only tears and confusion. My vacation time was spent on a rollercoaster of emotions. A fear of returning to my regularly scheduled program, only to have to explain why there are no newborn photos. When you're in a relationship and death hits home, you realize everyone grieves differently. My husband threw away all of the medication from day one, so I was left to feel. That's one thing I can say he saved me from. Although he self-medicated with marijuana, I was forced to feel everything. Just like the day I gave birth to my son. He watched, as I physically endured the pain. I had to return back to work, while my husband decided to party away his grief. We never spoke about what happened and pretended to be normal. For a few months it worked, but eventually we slowly started to disconnect further apart. In a way, this was the first time I made him feel needed. He was always around during the few months after me giving birth. He became the very man that I always knew he could be. He showed up, but didn't stick around long. It was nice while it lasted, but I guess that's why I went back every time. I was hoping he would show up...but he never did.

We got invited to a trip to Miami by one of his friends right around the time I returned to work. My mother told me I was a fool to let my man go to Miami all alone. With his track record, I was a fool to let him go to work, school, or outside for that matter. He was a serial cheater and I was aware. This was going to be my first time without him since London passed, but I wanted him to enjoy himself. He was disappointed but I had to care for our home. I was the breadwinner for our family. He barely kept a job longer than six months. I was always in school and working a decent paying job. Corrections was not my ideal career, but he suggested I go for it and I became a Correctional Officer. A pregnant officer that strolled the blocks, monitoring inmate's behaviors up until I was nine months. He left to Miami, and for the first time since the loss of my son, I was alone.

I had to learn to be on my own again, but I called him multiple times during his vacation. One particular time was to tell him some interesting news. He had hung up on me many times during the trip as he had returned to his college boy ways. This time I needed to tell him something that I myself was surprised about. "I'm pregnant." I said to my then husband vacationing in Miami. "What are you going to do?" was his response. I was confused, because after all we just went through, primarily I, he had the nerve to even suggest not having the baby. I couldn't believe his lack of empathy, but then again I wasn't surprised. Another pregnancy that was not celebrated Fuck him, I just went through hell and back delivering our stillborn son. I am not about to get rid of a child. He wasn't ready but I wasn't second guessing God's blessing. I had it in my mind that this relationship had been over, but now I had to focus on myself. I decided I will celebrate my pregnancy myself. I was going to make sure this new set of footprints would make it. Even if I had to endure it all alone. "I hope it is a girl!"

HEALING IN TEARS...

Everyone wants to be happy. I desire complete joy. I live for the moments that I am so filled with joy my cup overflows. Those moments are cherished because of the tears of sadness. How can those tiny salty droplets carry both our deepest sadness and joy? The droplets are similar to the rain that pours in storms with grey clouds, or a summer rain in daylight that creates the brightest rainbows.

RESEMBLANCE IN HIS HANDS...

One day, as I lay next to my husband before one of my grueling night shifts, he was asleep as usual especially now that he has been working a lot. I laid there with my eyes closed. My mind was running a mile a minute. Although he gets on my nerves most of the time, I swear nothing feels better than him holding me or vice versa. Today was different though. For some odd reason I felt so close to London. It was extremely warm outside today and even with the slight breeze we got coming through the windows, both of our bodies heat was too much for me. Seeing as how being pregnant again "Hot" had become my middle name due to my raging hormones. I swear getting dressed has become a workout for me. As I rolled over he reached out for me placing his hand on my hips to keep me near. I touched his hand as to reassure him that I wasn't going anywhere, at least for the next hour. As I touched his hand I felt his fingers and imagined London's hands. I always said since I met him how could such a small built guy have such large hands and feet. London had those same traits.

Everything about him was our son and I will always love him for that gift.

A NEW SET OF FOOTPRINTS...MICAH

Today is the day the lord has made. I know this because the joy I feel. It has been a while for me to wake up this early in the morning feeling like today was my day. Today felt like a gift. That it was exactly! I don't know how I could wake up feeling this way after sleeping on a close friend's sleeper couch that killed my back all night. I don't know if it was because this baby is about due or the damn couch was no good. Either way I was still feeling good back pains and all. My husband had me stay with our close Friends so that they could watch over me just in case something happened. They lived about a street away in a third floor apartment. It still beats my fourth floor. They just had their first about three weeks prior and I was due to go in for my induction. I didn't need no alarm or anyone else to wake me up. I was up like a kid excited for their first day of school. I woke up with a smile and it has been a while since that happened. My mood usually depended on my husband and how he was feeling, or what good news I was going to have today. Especially after what happened to me a year ago, smiles had become rare for me. At one point I laughed about it to my husband comparing myself to Wednesday from the movie "The Adams Family". Anytime that I would smile people were frightened. I actually scared myself by practicing my smile in the mirror. Something that is so natural had become something so foreign for me.

He came to pick me up from one of his night shifts at a retail store that he was working for the holidays. Luckily he had picked up this job right on time because money was going to be extremely tight. I burned through all my vacation and sick time last year so there was no money coming in on my part this time around. I still don't get it why we women have to use our vacation time on maternity leave as if we are going on vacation. Of course companies will never understand. Truly we are leaving one job to go to another. I feel bad for him because I know he wants the best for us, but ever since he got in to trouble, decent paying jobs have been hard to come by. It's been a rough road for the both of us but I just knew that this would be the day that would bring us together. Here we are almost exactly a year ago we lost our baby boy and now God was giving us a second chance. A second chance at life.

My husband walks in the door with a semi smile. It has also been a while since I have been the reason for that. So many things have gone on since we lost London and during this pregnancy that we have disconnected. He was a bit different this time around. He treated me as if I was fragile until I had showed him otherwise. He did not want to do anything, including sex. He wanted to be cautious trying to prevent the same thing happening twice. I kind of understood where he was coming from. He asked me how my night was and asked was I ready. Before I was nervous and acted as if I wasn't, but after experiencing that nightmare I know I could conquer anything. We headed home so we could pack and he could get a few hours of sleep before we headed to the hospital. I showered and had my hair freshly done the day before. The house was cleaned to my liking and everything was ready for the baby. This time around we did not have as much stuff as we had before for London. I have to blame myself for that. I gave it all away. I cleaned out his room thinking I could clean out my heart, my feelings, and my memories. They are all still there until today. I got all dolled up, fresh, and shaved to get ready. While he was sleeping I got in the car after debating on whether or not I was going to get a pedicure. I took one look down at my feet and decided it was a must. It was a fairly warm day for it to be November. I remember having the windows down and me blasting my music as I headed to one of my favorite nail salons. I recall about two other women sitting getting their nails done. They got me in and out. I headed back home with my windows down and my heat blasting on my feet just to make sure that my toes don't smudge. Way too many times after paying so much money for a pedicure I end up messing them up.

At home our bags were packed and ready to go sitting by the door. He got up to run a couple of errands and I sat home day dreaming and watching one of those medical shows. It was a marathon and Honestly, I never watched that show but it seemed to grab my interest that day. There was this one episode that came on right before it was time for me to check in to the hospital. It was of a woman having a baby and having to go for an emergency C-section. The woman died on the table and I sat there and cried. I bawled my eyes out. Literally as the show was ending my husband comes prancing through the door bright eyed.

The whites of his eyes tinted pink and he was sweet as ever. I knew he went and got high. He stopped smoking last year for about six months or so and was doing so well. Once we found out about London right before I gave birth   He left to get high right before I gave birth. Like I said I couldn't blame him he was scared and the weed always seemed to mellow him out. I didn't want him to go back to his old ways hanging out with people that don't mean him well. This time around he stayed away from most of the ones he got into trouble with before. Instead he smoked or hung out with an old high school friend that was really close to the both of us. I tugged at the waist of my maternity jeans to pull them up over my large belly.

Everything was already packed and ready to go and sitting at the door. This time around I just knew things would be different.

PAPERS…

The house felt so cold today. Even though it was twenty degrees outside, I don't think the frigid air was the type of cold I felt. I felt so alone, although physically I wasn't. My son Micah was there, but he wasn't. Mentally I have been torn down from the events from the past few years. Losing our son a year ago was the most traumatic of it all. But I just don't understand him. I stuck by his side for years. A lot of women would disagree with the amount of foolishness I tolerated. I felt empty. Here I am with the most amazing little boy God could have created and once again I felt as though something was missing. He left because once again, I kicked him out of "my house'. This time, being the fifth or sixth time. This time felt different though. I was hurt, but knew that I had to do something about it. I mean I love this man more than I love myself. That being the major problem. I have dealt with the multiple times he has cheated, lied, and deceived me. I have never judged him and remained as his confidant through his troubled times dealing with the court system. He was labeled so many times as the "bad guy" but I knew different. I knew of him as being very sensitive, caring, loving, and very attentive. Only thing is it hasn't been that way in a while. He tells me on a constant basis that he doesn't know how to love. To tell you the truth I don't think most of us do. Women come the closest being the nurturer and emotional creatures that we are. The greatest love story, which is in the bible, consists of God showing his love by sacrificing his only son. How can any of us compete with such a story? Knowing how to love I believe is something that does not need to be taught. It is a basic human need, a feeling we desire. Love is something that we can't see, nor taste, or touch but we all believe in it.

Until one day we get burned. How can someone say they don't know how to love? The day your first child is born the room is filled with it. You are overjoyed. I loved the fact that he was all of these things and more with our son, but what happened to me, your wife. Today I woke up to a beautiful smiling baby boy. After showering my son with kisses and hugs, I caught him out the corner of his eye looking at me but he never spoke. He knew that I was looking at him waiting for him to respond but he never did. I don't know if I was beginning to get used to the neglect but today was not the first day that he did not acknowledge me right in front of him. As usual he got up and began walking around the house as if to prepare for his day. Ever since I have met him he loved being out of the house. It was routine, as soon as his feet hit the floor he would prepare for his day. I enjoyed that about him. It was like him being a child all over again with the excitement of a new day. Only thing was I did not feel a part of that.

Three months after we lost London there was such a huge disconnect. I felt, as I had to make the first move or be the first to greet in the morning. If I did not take the initiative then I could forget being spoken to. I felt as though I had died along with London in so many ways. So today was another initiative day. I guess once again I had to open my mouth and say something. "You can't say good morning?" was my response to the earlier ignoring session. Little did I know that it was possibly the wrong thing to say. Obviously at that point he did not want to be bothered and me questioning him was not a part of his agenda. It has been a couple of months that I felt him being distant. I would speak to him and he would completely ignore me or act as if I wasn't even standing in front of him. I would be a millionaire if I had a dollar for all the times I had to ask him if he heard what I said. I honestly can say I felt like he hated me. I would come home from work happy for one, it was a new day and for two, to see my two favorite people. Like he tells me constantly he just did not make me his priority. I truly understand people wanting time to themselves, but when in a relationship the other partner will eventually feel neglected. Sad to say but now that I think of it most of the times it annoyed him with me asking him questions in general. I am the type of individual that wants to talk about the situation at hand right then and there. I have learned though that everyone handles things differently and he was the type to walk away from the problem and then address it when he was ready. This was also one of the big issues in our relationship.

I wanted to fix and mend everything and he wanted to hold a grudge and continue on with his day. Of course, I continued on and on about how or why it's such a problem for him to greet me in the mornings or be a little more attentive. He on the other hand felt as though the situation was minor and that I was nagging him as usual. I began to become frustrated at his nonchalant attitude towards my feelings and he just got more and more annoyed. He then walked into our son's room and grabs a stack of fresh papers that he had stored in one of his sneaker boxes. I was looking at him as to what he could possibly be doing. Once he got the papers he threw them on our living room floor and said, "If you don't like it then do something about it." Flashback to just a week ago we just had a sit down discussion about the status of our relationship. He just recently moved back in and just had one of his famous smoking sessions in which it allowed him to tolerate a conversation with me. Of course I sat there pouring my heart out as usual about how I feel and what things we could do to improve our relationship. I could tell how much he hated these conversations but they were important to me.

Normally I try to touch base on every aspect of the relationship including asking him how I could improve our sex life. Although our son was three months old we completely went past the six-week mark. I don't even think he even looked at me in that way physically. A week before the conversation we were lovebirds trying to bring back the romance. It was the first time we had sex and it was two times in one night. I finally felt sexy or like a woman. That came to an end when we had spoken about our sex life when he stated "It's boring."

I mean throughout my pregnancy I constantly addressed my need to still feel close and to fulfill my personal desires. Yes we women also have a sex drive. He just seemed very nonchalant. I mean I googled lack of sex during pregnancy curious as to see who else has dealt with this. It's interesting that there are a pretty high percentage of men that are either one afraid of hurting the baby, or two are turned off by the weight gain. I guess losing our son had a lot to do with it also and we were afraid that it could happen again but my doctor never said refrain from sex. So here I was listening to him tell me everything that I do wrong as usual. Just like men we have an ego and we want it to be stroked. Just an fyi, having sex and making your wife feel loved opens up doors and excitement in the bedroom. The more confident that your spouse feels the freakier (I think I made this word up) or adventurous your sex life will be. Honestly the most excitement that I got through my pregnancy was reading fifty shades of grey. Our relationship was at its lowest point and divorce was coming up in conversations very often. So back to the papers that were tossed at me that was lying on the floor. I already consciously knew what the papers were but in my mind I couldn't believe that he would have the nerve.

Did he really just throw divorce papers at me after everything we have just went through and all the hard work I had put into this relationship? When did he go and get them? Obviously he had them stored in that box so what was he waiting for? Once again my soul was torn. I felt my blood rushing through my body and my stomach plummeted. How could he? Throwing divorce papers at me meant that either I was right about how I felt, which believe me all of us have a huge sense of intuition. If it doesn't seem right it isn't right. Once again it goes back to me and my saying "You can say you love me until your face is black and blue, but your actions are what truly matters." I gave you two beautiful children, supported him through his life trials, and have given this man all my love. This is how he fucking repays me. I signed it.

SINGLE BLACK MOTHER…

I always said that I would be a single parent. I guess that was me screaming independent, but in all honesty it is hard doing it all alone. Then again, in my family, this was the norm. I remember always being told that a baby will never make a man want to stay with you, but I thought our circumstances were different. I thought that he was going to be our miracle baby and that you would appreciate me even more after he was born. Instead of seeing me through your everyday view that just maybe you would look at me as your strong and amazing wife. I did it. I went through another pregnancy, held my head high, and delivered a healthy baby boy for us. It isn't just you though, it's me as well. I have a problem with how I view myself. Now I know that I cannot expect others to see things the way that I view them or to see me as I see myself. I was my own worst enemy. You were just the cosigner.

SEARCHING FOR ANSWERS...

I know for me that particular situations place me on a path to search for answers. Every time I attend a funeral, or experience a loss, I go months thinking about life and my purpose. When my son was born stillborn, I wanted answers. I wanted answers from the physicians, my ex-husband, my family and friends. I wanted God to reveal to me the reason for my pain. I was angry with the world but hid behind a smile. My depression was masked by my ability to do my daily task. I have engaged in church, counseling and hypnotherapy. Yes, I have tried it all. It is so much easier to have faith when life is going well. When you're in the storm and your faith is being tested this is a whole other story. I have been on the healing path for more than five years now and within the last year have engaged in some interesting spiritual healing. I was in Manyunk, an artsy section of Philadelphia having dinner with one of my girlfriends. I am going to refer to her as Kim. Kim and I enjoyed drinks and dinner at this Cajun restaurant and decided to head to insomnia cookies for dessert. We were walking and discussing the usual, life and relationships and walked directly past our desired destination. We came across a palm reading sign that said $10 palm reading outside of a clairvoyant residence.

I have always enjoyed following Silvia Brown and learning about psychics but never had a reading for myself. I was doing well in the healing process but really wanted to find out where my life was going. I randomly came across the Pharma industry after my move here to Pennsylvania, and recently got divorced. I was trying to date and really just wanted to know where my life was headed. I also wanted to get in touch with my grandmother and see if she was proud of me and the woman I have become. I was curious but extremely nervous at the same time. I think the biggest fear of seeing a psychic is them telling you that you're near death. I mean death is inevitable, but for some odd reason we all live life as if it isn't. The idea of knowing scares most of us, but at this point I was a little tipsy and fear was drowning in the martini I had for dinner. We walked in the shop which was bright and surrounded by the color purple with books of tarot and spiritual information. The woman who greeted us was heavy-set with long black hair and a soft-spoken voice. She proceeded to introduce herself and tell us about the tarot readings and the cost. Michelle the clairvoyant mentioned the different types of things her shop did spiritually and speaking to the dead was one of them. She stated that she usually doesn't do that for a first time reading but Kim and I decided this was something that I needed to do. The reading ran $125 or something so I had to go get cash from a local ATM.

As we walked to get the cash Kim asked me how I felt about doing the reading. I told her I wanted to see if this was true and if I could contact my son or grandmother. I was excited and even if the experience wasn't what I expected I was fine with losing the money. Kim left me at the shop, and went home because Michelle stated she wouldn't be able to focus on my energy and the energy of my loved ones if she attended. She proceeded to take me downstairs to a beautifully decorated room with a chaise, and a desk with a bench. She sat me down and asked me for my hands. As she took my hands and peered into my heart and soul, she told me things about my life that I wouldn't expect for her to know and she began this by telling me my past life regression. According to Michelle, I am an old soul; a lonely soul that has never been family oriented and has never found their soul mate. I am a tired soul and I have an open window in which my past lives affect the current life I am in. My previous curiosity may have heightened my beliefs but much of what she said brought light to me and my current life. I cried the ugly cry as everything seemed so relative and made me see why I behave the way I do. She mentioned that I had three previous lives in which she was able to see. The first life she stated I was a young Asian girl. One of which was a sex slave that died by being strangled. She stated this was the reason for my interest in Buddhism and Asian culture. That young girl resides in me and affects my current life through my intimacy issues and timid ways sexually. She also explained my fear of not breathing and short breaths. She stated I currently breathe just enough to live. She recognized something within me I barely recognized myself. I was lost for words. She began then to tell me about my second life, I was a warrior, which meant I was a man....

To be continued....

SEARCHING FOR ANSWERS...TRUST

The window into my current life was a mockery of the one Michelle was explaining to me now. She proceeded to tell me that in another past life, I was a warrior. My current life was an example of a warrior. My physical and spiritual strength potentially could be a result to this life she was now addressing. She stated that in this life I was a loner. Not much family or love for that matter. I was laughing as she explained to me that I was a man, but very caring and sensitive. I never found true love in this life as well, and was killed on the battlefield. The story behind my death is what still burdens me. I was supposedly on the battlefield, when I noticed a young child in the midst of the violence. I stopped and tried to redirect the child to safety. Michelle proceeded to tell me that when I turned my back the child stabbed me and I died instantly. The compassion and concern for the child lead me to lose my life. The unexpected wound to the back from a child, has led me on the path with a lack of trust in others. This has carried on with me as well into my current life. Michelle also decided to tell me that since I was a man in my previous life that I show interest in women physically. I mean this is something that I thought about to myself, and was surprised when she mentioned this to me (or knew about). I don't ever see myself in a relationship with a woman; however the sexual curiosity was there. She told me that I wasn't attracted to people but more attracted to souls... which lead unto my last life as the healer.

My last life she said I was a healer and did natural homeopathic healing. This made the connection for me in regards to my love for crystals, aromatherapy, and many other natural remedies. She went on to explain to me that my life as a healer has made me susceptible to attract broken souls. The life of the healer lasted only until about sixty. To be honest, I forgot how she said I passed on in that life. Now I'm sitting there with my mouth open looking at Michelle astonished at what she was telling me. She proceeded to tell me that she knew how tired my soul was and she was wondering why I choose to keep coming back. I'm not saying that everything that Michelle told me was true, but in that moment, she spoke to my soul. My soul cried that day; it wasn't the tears of Kieona. It was the tears of someone who has traveled many paths searching for answers. Now that I think of it, do my previous lives make me question my faith and trust in the process? She never mentioned to me whether or not my past lives were fulfilled, but there is something different about this one. I have a son, who was actually my best friend in a previous life, who spiritually and emotionally connects with me in a way no one else has. He emotional fills holes and knows what I need before I even say. He actually saved my life.

Michelle mentioned to me my life's purpose of saving other women, because I once was stuck in the dark of depression and suicidal. My sons brought back my light and trust in God's plans. Michelle told me that my grandmother was making an appearance but was reluctant to speak with her because she didn't believe she did what she did. Right then, I knew that was my grandmother. Michelle told me that my grandmother decided to take the path as a guardian angel and has watched over me and the family ever since. Michelle kept apologizing for the things she was saying but my grandmother had no filter. She was a blunt woman and Michelle said she reminded her of Madea. Bingo! My grandmother kept referencing the feather/angel wing that I have on my left arm that I placed on her tombstone. That was her way of saying thank you. Now every time that I see it, I know I am where I'm supposed to be with her guidance. My grandmother told Michelle that her fear is for me to raise Micah alone. She said she was getting upset about me doing everything myself and she wanted to see me in a happy, healthy relationship. She said she always knew that I was the one in the family to break the generational curse. This curse occurs amongst many African-American families. She knew I was the one prepared to change the mindset of the women before me and to live in my purpose. Michelle told me what God's vision for me was. I would share it but I rather show you. My mother's life before I was created and the life of my father and his sins was the fluid I marinated in for nine months. My Mother never really shared the story of my conception but I was made aware of the broken relationship between her and my father. She didn't have to tell me much because I relived it and seen it with my own eyes when I was pregnant with London. I sympathize so much for others because I know pain all too well. I decided that day that I wanted to close the chapters of my past lives, and move towards my purpose. It wasn't going to be easy I had more work to do but it was beyond the physical. I had mental and spiritual work to do...a fight between heaven and hell (positive and negative energy) on top of all the other daily things I do. While I continue on the search for answers...

ANSWERS IN A BOOK

After losing London, I read every "how to achieve happiness" book you could think of. I desired something. I came to the conclusion that you will never find the answers in the pages of another person's book. There you will find the tools and guidance to aide you in your journey. Your journey is your very own unique chapters of your book. As I believe every soul has a story to tell.

SACRIFICE...

To sacrifice is an act of surrendering a prized possession. Be careful because sacrificing can lead to resentment if it is done with the wrong intent, and not done in love. Some people sacrifice themselves and surrender themselves solely to their partner, children, and careers. All while giving their all and neglecting themselves. So to all the people that fall victim to giving not in love but for someone else's pleasure, you will be greatly disappointed in the end. After all you have done, only to hear "I never asked you to do that!" How stupid of me, to give someone something that I didn't even give to my damn self. My time, my love, and my self- appreciation, were all things I didn't give to myself. If I neglected to do so for myself, what makes me think the next person wouldn't do so as well?

MANIFEST...

I guess I can say that I have reached an all-time low. No I am not on drugs and need an intervention, nor have I experienced a severe break down. Dammit, I am pretty close. I swear I thought I had it bad during my young adolescent days. I struggled through middle school because of everything that went on with the family. Like middle school wasn't hard enough. Then dealing with high school and trying to find myself, which ten years later at the age of twenty eight I am still in that process. I guess it is better for me to endure my trials and tribulations now, rather than at a later stage in life. I remember while I was staying with my father on Amity court in the big blue house. My room would face the yard. Now this was not your average yard with a lot of grass or space. I honestly felt bad for my father's dog because he really didn't have much space to roam. It was like the size of a studio apartment. One more body or dog placed back there it would have been too crowded. Luckily he didn't seem to mind. In fact he was quite content. The yard was surrounded by a wooden gate that separated an auto body shop and the house. There was this huge tree that I believe was on the auto body shops part but its huge branches fell over to our side of the gate. There was nothing special about this tree except for the fact that I liked looking at it. It did not have special flowers growing from it or fruit. It was just this huge ordinary tree. Just like every other teenager I had spent a lot of time in my room. Most of this time consisted of doing homework and listening to music. Every day though, I would take time out to stare out the window at this ordinary yet huge tree. Many times I was praying out to god while staring into the universe or the sky. Asking God to send me now what I think is ridiculous blessings but back then seemed essential. Asking some popular guy in school to finally notice me and ask me out like the high school movies I would watch. Or to give me big boobs like one of my best friends whom I envied because of her grown woman curves. These were my worries or my troubles that at that age were stressful. Now I wish I still had those same issues. All the while when I would stop praying or begging God for my selfish nonsense I would observe the basic tree.

I resided in that room for a total of four or five years and that tree remained in the same exact spot also. The interesting thing about the tree as I look back and think about it now was it was a symbol of me. Now I know you're thinking how a tree can be a symbol of a human being. That tree like clockwork was constantly changing. Changing along with every season and watching this tree allowed me to realize how quickly time passes. How time waits for no one or nothing. Like clockwork that same tree or just like any other would conform or adjust to the changing seasons. My favorite part was when the buds began to form on the tree. It was a sense of newness that there was going to be a new beginning. This meant more sun light and longer days, warmer weather and new challenges. No matter what the weather would bring that tree stood there. Tall, strong, and unique in its own particular ways. That tree for me symbolized a pattern, of growth, learning, falling and getting up again. It symbolized a pattern.

Here I was praying to God while staring out into the universe with my selfish prayers and he or the universe was placing a response right in front of my face. I never realized that my insecurities and confidence issues were just the beginning to my story. This tree standing in front of my window was a symbol of a repetitious cycle that I would have to endure from my adolescent years to my young adulthood. A cycle that has affected my life so much that I had to sit down and write about it. Every year just like that tree I would grow, fall, and grow again. Whether through rain, sleet, hail, hurricane, earthquake, or even a tornado I AM STILL STANDING. Just like the old saying "fair weather friends" I have had a handful of those. The ones who enjoyed your company while everything was good, but once the storm came you couldn't find them. It's sad to say, but I can even say that I have had family members that I can classify as these individuals.

Looking out my window of my home I bought a year ago while in my bedroom, I just felt like I had déjà vu. When I was a teenager living in my father's house, I had a window similar to the one I have now. That window back at my father's did not have much of a view, but the huge tree also caught my attention. I used to sit and watch the tree change over the years. Staying rooted into who it was but shedding leaves and growing new ones as the seasons changed. My room was plastered with clippings from magazines about fashion, places I would love to go, and people I would love to meet. In that room, I felt trapped. I was stuck and that window, tree, and my music were my way to escape. My music, writing, and a lust for something different helped me make it through the challenges I faced within that home. I felt like I was a burden all my life. Never really ever felt wanted. Being between both parents house, I never really felt home. Sitting here writing almost 18 years later, I am back in that same space again. The same space of wanting to relocate to somewhere I believe love lives. Giving up everything I know to start all over. I am exhausted with giving so much of myself to prove to people that I am worthy of being loved. Everything that teenager once dreamed became her reality. Every thought both positive and negative I manifested.

I got married, had children, and a career by the age of 30, but I did it my way. I forced things to work for me instead of allowing it to happen in divine time. Looking out of the window of my current home at a trail full of tress, I am now divorced, lost a child, and have experienced tumultuous relationships with both family, friends and men. I truly believe none of this would have happened if I would have stuck to my plans of marrying Usher. Okay, just kidding but really. I had plans on living happily ever after; you know that fairy tale shit. I went against my intuition and connection with God and forced love and other situations only to end up with heartache. As a teenager, I was stuck in the pain of my childhood. Unworthiness and insecurities were the foundation I was planted on. A week ago I realized that all the healing that I had done, was not as sturdy as I thought it was. I spent the last two years alone/single, working on myself. I traveled, lost and gained friends and focused on bettering myself. Unconsciously, I was stuck in the pain. I wanted a family and would do anything to have and keep one. Obviously my desires for this stemmed from the lack of family throughout my childhood. I wanted to know what it would have been like if my mother took my father back when he decided to rid himself of his heroin addiction. I was forced to understand her past through experiencing loving a man incapable of loving me. The little girl in me told me to wait for my husband because if your father changed, then one day he will too.

The evolved woman says there is too much hurt and we both no longer want the same things. Some say it's a Taurus thing to stick it out as long as you can when it comes to a relationship we are extremely loyal yet stubborn. The little girl in me did not want to give up on him like my mother did my father. I understand now as she believed she was doing what was right for her at that time. In the end she did leave my father, but she kept falling in love with the same kind of man, except for different physical appearances. We may change the relationship and the people we are involved with, but if we don't do the inner work our experiences won't change. I have only been in two and half relationships in my life. Don't ask me what that means. There have been men in between but I attracted similar circumstances. I attracted people who were seeking or needed healing. I gave these men what I believed was unconditional love. A love I believed actually existed but was unwilling to give it me. A love with no boundaries, or expectations. I was giving them the love I had wished I received as a child. The more I loved without conditions, the more disrespectful they became. They knew that I would always take them back as they had no fear of loss or consequences when it came to playing with my heart. I did not love myself. I told myself I did, but I didn't. Actions speak louder than words. I am still working on this…hence the fact I am still single.

Like the tree at my father's house, and the trees along the trail of my current home I have remained rooted. The inequities and sins of those before me have been imprinted on the roots of my tree. I have shed relationships like the leaves in fall, and blossomed new leaves when the seasons changed. No matter where I have gone, whether Springfield or Pennsylvania, I could not run from myself. Massachusetts was the grieving state; Pennsylvania provided my resources to healing. I can't escape the thoughts of guilt and being unworthy without studying the reason for it in the first place. I wanted an escape from this house. I wanted to leave. Now that I think about it I always ran away from the very things or places that hurt me. I left out of fear. Don't leave out of fear, leave in purpose. Who was I before life first broke me…I'm not running anymore.

LEAVING IN FEAR...

I am not her. As I watched the movers finally help me unload the rest of my belongings out of the truck, I recall igniting a conversation to remind complete strangers that "I am not her." In reality, I was not trying to prove anything to them, it was more for me. I had a reputation to keep, and a standard of living that I managed to uphold. This is only temporary, I would repeat to the movers as I gave them direction to where I desired for my belongings to be placed. It wasn't like they had much of an option. I went from a 3,000 square foot home to a one bedroom less than 800 sq. ft. I made up my mind that I was going to relocate, even if that meant for me to give up everything. I sold most of my belonging and even gave most of my furniture to my tenants. An almost two thousand dollars couch for their dog to lie on. It bothered me at one point, but if it cost me my freedom, I would give a thousand more times over. I stripped myself of everything. Just to start anew. I have made some unconscious decisions, or decisions I later realized were out of fear or avoidance. That home I bought wasn't done for me, it was to finally prove him and everyone else that I could do it. The only problem with proving to others your ability, the rewards are only temporary. When you do something for yourself, to prove to others, it will not be sustained. Telling the movers "I am not her" was me finally realizing I never knew who she was. My decision to relocate was me running away from the very place that almost broke me. I wasn't leaving here in Love, I was leaving in fear.

FLOWERS...

It all started with a bouquet of roses and a hanging flower arrangement for my home. A nice bottle of red wine and a whispered promise of dreams I once had. I held unto those dear flowers for my life, as they were the first gifts I received after all the pain. That night I was seen through the eyes I wished would remain for the rest of my life. The eyes of appreciation for the life I gave, and the woman I had become. With time those flowers began to wilt, and today was the day I finally threw them out. I wasn't consistent and neither was he. The flowers would go days without water but withstood the summer and high heat. Those beautiful flowers began to wilt because the love and care just wasn't something I could give. I would go days without remembering to care for them. They just weren't my priority. I gave up on the plant because I am not the one with a green thumb. My ability to care or acknowledge the importance of greenery has just never been my thing. I appreciated its beauty when they were nicely cared for, but disliked its appearance when the petals became wilted. I gave up on continuing to breathe life into that plant. Now I understand there are just some things people are incapable of doing. Today, I saw its potential of what it could be, if I only invested time in watering it properly. Filling it up with water and light, just to see it grow and flourish. Instead I made a choice. I made a choice to throw it away and start over. I will stick with the fake plants for now since they are easier to care for. Now I see why he did not choose me. I needed light and love and that was too much of a distraction from what he was used to. I required from him, something he was unable to provide me at the time. In the end, he threw it all away. He decided that the fake flowers, the ones that withstand his lack of emotions and care are good for now. It all started with flowers and a bottle of red wine. I never ask for much. The things I require should come naturally. My petals began to weep, and once he threw me away, I had no choice but to start all over again. Flowers

INTENTIONS...

He told me what his intentions were this time around. I can't believe I even thought to take him back after divorcing me for the women he left me for. Like all the other situations in my life , I thought I could control how he felt about me, or change his mind. This time around, I thought he was different because he seemed to be able to appreciate me more after losing me. All the women he cheated with were very different from me. I was home to him, nurturing and comforting. I was the mother he wanted but lacked as a child. They were the vacations, all confident and carefree. I kept fighting myself finally to realize that what we were doing was just entertainment for him. He needed a release, and having sex with me just confirmed that I was "never going anywhere". Sex to him was just a thing. To me, we became even more spiritually connected. His intentions weren't good, not just for me but also for himself. Every time life got hard for him he knew where to go. To a place where he could abuse the

unconditional love of a selfless woman. He would always come
HOME...

CHECK IN...

Do me a favor...I don't need you to check in! You made a decision to step out of my life knowing I had abandonment issues. Yes, I am responsible for leaving the door cracked that should have smacked you in the ass when you left. Now you got your big ass head peeking through to see who is responsible for making me smile. I'm sure you have become a fan of my pictures on Facebook and blog post that may have mentioned you. I don't need fans. Fans are people that love what you do for them not loving you for who you are. You said you always wanted what's best for me but I believe that's a lie. What's best for me was a life without you and your negativity. Anything that brings confusion is really not good for you. My happiness sparked your interest. I was living a life of happiness without you and you became intrigued. As a energy sucker you wanted to be filled, filled with the joy of life God instilled in me. You were confused as to why I was not torn. You did everything in your will to break me and I still prevailed. You even had a team of energy suckers that were unsuccessful.

I blame myself for leaving a thimble of hope. A small piece of faith that you will recognize the woman that was in front of you. Yeah she fucked you over, and showed you what crazy really is ... so you decided to check in on me. Last time I checked you don't have a PhD, or any degree for that matter. You have always lacked empathy and concern for others. Your selfish ways were more concerned for my joy without you. So since your conducting check ins, write yourself a prescription, a medicine for awareness and accountability. Maybe even a pill for amnesia for the both of us. Because for just a second I forgot the pain you brought and you the damage you done. No need to check in...

EPIPHANY...

He said he couldn't see his life without me…but his epiphany of us wasn't aligned with my dream of what we could be…so I had to let him go. I was the woman that fed him intellectually, challenged his thoughts, while the others fulfilled his sexual cravings. A woman of substance is hard to come by, in a society full of savages. I had to let him go as a reminder for him, and a confirmation of strength for me.

BELIEVER...

That man doesn't feel worthy of your love...or worthy of you. This is shown through his mixed signals and your confusion.

Trust...

You can't make someone believe what they deserve. Making him a believer is not your job.

SORRY...

Sorry is a term that I loosely use for my insecurities, and to be honest the reason I use it is because it appears to work or ease complicated situations. I am the girl that apologizes for just about everything. I even apologize for others mistakes just to make the other person feel better about their behavior in the situation. Yes! I carry the burden and the weight on my shoulders but never fully understood the term and why it is used so loosely. There are countless songs using the term as the title to express sympathy for another. Or as Bryson Tiller would put it "Sorry not Sorry". Phrases to sugar coat the fact that you could really care less to sympathize for another. Yet many of us yearn for the day to receive this one worded expression to be left with more healing and understanding amongst ourselves. The term sorry is defined as a feeling of distress, especially through sympathy with someone else's misfortune. My question is what if the misfortune was caused by the person now sympathizing? Is sorry a word created to compensate an untaken evaluation of one's own insecurities and responsibilities? Is it a way of smoothing things over. This term is used across all relationships whether coworkers, parents and children, and especially intimate relationships. Or is it a way for one to finally let someone know they have acknowledge their behavior?

The events leading up to the term being used loosely can be extremely emotionally costly. Costly enough to leave you questioning its value and the lack of fairness in regards to what each party may have lost. I am recently divorced as of Sept. 2016 but the relationship was rocky for a very long time. Possibly it was rocky from the day it started. I saw the signs of heartbreak, but believed that my love could potentially change him. Well I was wrong! Fast forward...two children later and a marriage of four years and he left for one of my previous campers. (Yes, I was her camp counselor) A year and some change after splitting and ugly court proceedings I began picking myself up from where he left me. This was one of my lowest points of my life. I gained my strength and independence back and finally got back on my own two feet. Six months after the divorce I have graduated from my undergrad, started Grad school, bought my first home, traveled to Dominican Republic and Disney for Christmas. All done in the span of six to eight months of me focusing on me. During the whole time I just wanted him to acknowledge his wrongdoings. Actually I wanted to just hear the word "Sorry".

A few weeks ago the "Sorry" came and went. The heavens did not open up and the angels did not come pouring down singing as I'd hoped for. I knew it took a lot for him to say the word but I don't think he realized the blood sweat and tears it took me to be able to accept his word. His word "Sorry" lead to my action of evaluating me and continuing the healing process. As I'm always known for saying ...at the end of the day don't wait for the word "sorry". Apologize to yourself and begin the appropriate actions to change your frame of mind. We are responsible for our own actions and we play a tremendous role in how others treat us. "Sorry" is not the end it is the beginning of the forgiveness process and it all starts with you. The word doesn't make the pain disappear it is an acknowledgement that something hurt you. I will take my "sorry" payments in actions from now on!

THE AFTERMATH OF FORGIVENESS...

Just like other things in life forgiveness is a process. It requires more than the actual action of forgiving. Like apologizing, forgiving is just the beginning. When someone hurts you, the level of hurt all depends on your reaction to the person's behavior. The more you love someone, the more pain they potentially can cause. The problem I am having when it comes to forgiveness is meeting the person where they are now. When I decide to forgive someone, I decide to let go of the past. I decided to let go of the pain they caused and whatever negativity came with them. Pain is not only caused by people who don't love you, but it can come from those who do. So what happens when those people resurface or re-enter your life? We all have the choice to have certain people around us but sometimes there are those who are always around, like close family. It is imperative within the process to let go (forgive) the past behaviors of the individual, and meet the person they are presenting to you right now. I'm starting to believe that I have PTSD, not a severe case, but one in which circumstances trigger negative thoughts and response from me. the behavior of the other individual may just be similar to what has occurred before and leads me to assume an outcome or create my own negative scenario. Everything around us changes, including people. Most people have the desire to evolve and have learned lessons from their past mistakes. Create a clean slate within your mind that allows you to create new memories with them, as opposed to the pain and hurt of the past. To forgive is the emotional commitment to let go for not only the pain of another but for your emotional wellbeing. A commitment requires a level of work that many of us don't acknowledge necessary. To forgive is the first step, but there is work in the aftermath. Work that requires you to let go of what you thought you knew about someone, and to be open to who is standing in front of you today!

INTIMATE PAIN...

The same way he catapulted me out of the marriage, is the same way he reminded me off my purpose. The same two hands of resemblance of something pure, wrapped around my neck. His eyes full of anger piercing through mine. This was the most eye contact I received from him throughout our relationship. How intimate was the pain he inflicted. The pain I accepted and believed I deserved. His continuous threats and wishes of me lifeless. I don't recall if my breathing was restricted, but in that moment I allowed him to take my power. This time was different, because I refused to fight back. I just wanted this to end. In a matter of seconds my life had changed. That very moment he confirmed my healing process was nowhere near finished. That my desire for family and love outside of myself was greater than my purpose. At that moment, he conquered the strong woman of color. The very movement that I created to inspire women, I became a contradiction to. That man that saw me give birth to two of his children. Who watched me give birth to our lifeless son, wished me dead.

RETURNED TO PIECES...

I have allowed people to take the better pieces of me to build…while I was left with a puzzle only I could put back together.

FEAR OF HAPPINESS...

Have you ever been so happy that it frightened you to the point you would not allow yourself to enjoy the moment? That your soul has become so inclined and receptive to negative energy. I'm a giver so I have to learn to receive and as I sat down in my car and evaluated where I am now as opposed to where I was a year ago. I cried because I realized that God has never failed me. There have been a lot of people who have walked out of my life over the past few years. I decided to hold people accountable as I do so for myself. I asked what did I do to deserve your mercy and he reminded me of my heart. Where I was years ago was all a reflection of how I felt about myself. Everything that I have done over the years in regards to accolades is minimal. My true strength lies in me being a fallen soul that stood and rose alone only to lend my hand to others. I am not bitter; I am better and have learned that my changes have inspired others. I have been hurt and continued to love. I gave life even after it was taken from me. I know this may seem harsh but Fuck anyone who doesn't like the improved me. The one that knows her worth and won't settle for less. Don't take my heart or kindness for weakness. Shit after everything I have experienced, I laugh at fear because I know once it subsides and I get out of my comfort zone, and happiness will be there to remind me it has been here all along. All I need is within me!

SURRENDER...

I surrender! When I say I surrender, I am referring to allow things to come and go. I am letting go of the need to control and taking responsibility over only my actions. I am ceasing the need to force things. I will not force relationships or things I believe that should occur. I have come to the understanding that I am not in total control. My words and my thoughts are the blueprint to what I want out of life. Everything that I have asked for, I have always received. Surrender to the process and open your eyes to the people, and events that occur in your life. There is no such thing as coincidences, everything happens on purpose, for your purpose. Where you are right now is preparing you for where you are about to go. Many of the things that I asked for, I didn't realize I received my request until I lost it. Too much is given, much is required. We ask for marriage and many times for the process, but have you shaped and prepared yourself for this? You want to become a parent, but have you taken the time to work on you? Being a parent is teaching another being how to travel through this journey called life. I forced relationships and allowed men back in my life confusing their selfishness and interest with love. I forced relationships just because I didn't want to be alone. Forcing relationships because I believed they brought value to me. "Slow down life is beautiful" a man told me while I was rushing to pick up my pizza during a lunch break. This man never met me before but saw everything that I did in that moment was a rush. He was right and anyone that knows me has seen how hectic my life is especially as a single mother. I went back home repeating this to myself. I am constantly going, from the time I wake up until the time I go to bed. Every goal I have set and achieved came and went. So now I surrender to the path that is set for me. One that I plan to enjoy along the way.

BITTER BLACK B$%^&...

According to my Ex, I would be the poster child for the definition of a "Bitter Black Bitch"! Like she said in the movie 'Diary of a mad Black woman', "I'm not bitter, I'm Mad as hell!" Why is it that when a black woman is disappointed or angry she has to be given a derogatory or demeaning label? Are we not entitled to self-expression? I have experienced it not only in relationships but also within the work place. Is it because I am opinionated and say what's on my mind? Is it because you find me intimidating because of my melanin and strong disposition? I learned a long time ago, not to expect people to do as I do, but what happened to do unto others. Some Black men are beginning to use the word "bitch" way too loosely, and as women we need to stop accepting these references. Am I bitter because of my dreams of you as my black man...failed? Am I bitter because I held you to a certain caliber as I do for myself? Am I bitter because I wanted different, for myself, for us and our child? I was let down through your continuous infidelity, while I maintained our home.

I gave up everything including my career believing that we could make our family work. I was Olivia Pope, fighting for you in the justice system while working and going to school. Patti Labelle making sure you got your nutrition, while still trying to be "bad" and a mother to our child. I may not have had the example of the picture perfect marriage, but I knew what love looked and felt like. I spent years playing the role of your mother, while depriving myself of a healthy meaningful relationship. If bitter is the term used for my disgust for your excuses. For every reason why everything you do is only a "try". I'm trying to be better through surrounding yourself with the same crowd, and barely holding down a full-time job. Never giving yourself time from relationships because the need is not love, you're a materialist. You're someone whose soul is empty but defines themselves by lavish things. A man who has never taken the time to find himself can never lead his family. So while you parade the town that I moved to, for you, with the next girl and her two children. I must have the conversations with my four-year old son, about what he observes is wrong. While being confused as to why you attend their sports events, when you haven't even made your presence known for your own. Or while your supporting a household with two children and not coming through for yours. I am disappointed because I held you responsible for making sure you do for yours first. That you would choose a partner that would make you a better man. Someone that holds you accountable for being a role model to all the children, instead of only there for hers. Instead you choose someone who has no expectations of you. Your disrespect for the mother of your child is observed by your child. Then there are the women that find their man disrespecting another woman amusing, they are beyond clueless. Your insecurities exude throughout your portrayal of extreme confidence...or lack of. I was his wife and the women that gave him two children, if he doesn't respect me, eventually what do you think he will do to you as a girlfriend?

I am angry that my son has to see his single black mother's strength and question his fathers. At the tender age of only four feeling a need to protect and provide. I guess bitter is the new better, because I had to pick up the pieces that you broke. I had to turn our house back into a home! I thank you for leaving me because I faced my fear of being alone. You reminded me that I could make it alone. The problem is, this generation of "Bitter Black bitches" we are becoming too independent. The trauma created by some of our black men that we love, leave us with broken hearts. We carry the world on our shoulders, but there is always a tiny space in our hearts for the black man. As you can see the black woman is on a rise. We "bitter black bitches" turned our anger into degrees, businesses, and became over achievers. While many of our black men are remaining stuck. Stuck trying to find themselves, and hurting every woman they come across because they are afraid of themselves. After a certain age we all become accountable for our growth. With that being said, I take responsibility for who I decided to plant my seed with. As young black girls we are taught that relationships are hard but you just got to work through it. Love is not a struggle! It comes with ease but chose your battles.

Disrespect, emotional abuse, physical abuse, cheating, lying, and deceit are things that will try to kill your soul. Be mindful that it is all a reflection of how you as a woman feel about yourself. I got angry when he called me this and lashed out in disbelief. This same man that saw me lose a child five years ago, had the nerve to perk his lips up to say this to the mother of his now four year old son. I am disappointed but I'm only responsible for my own role I play in this movie. So I will not feed into the negativity and the naysayers, Like my grandmother always said "They talked about Jesus, what makes you think they won't talk about you!" Once I feed into your words, I am accepting them. I'm not bitter, I'm better. Better now that you left. Since you left I have gained so much clarity. So while you continue to build a relationship that started off with a fucked up foundation. I am building a foundation for my son that is beyond material. One of love, forgiveness, kindness, patience and all coming from the "bitter black bitch!"

CHILD SUPPORT?

My mother was always concerned for me because she believed that I was more book smart than street smart. That theory of me no longer remains. I have always been an extremely emotional person and have even considered myself an "empath". I would pride myself on my emotions, and still feel strongly about the importance of them. They are our internal indicators, but sometimes can result in poor decision-making and affect our logical thinking. Today was Deja vu of exactly what my life was like in 2016. Only this time, I was proactive and not reactive. See people tend to forget about this university called life. Just like school, every lesson you are required to graduate from before moving on to the next stage. Many people are experiencing Groundhog Day instead with other people and differing events, but similar lessons to be learned. I was stuck in the pain and reopened the wound this summer only to repeat and be time warped back to 2016 the year of my divorce. 2016 was the time my ex-spouse decided to move another woman from my hometown to the very place he uprooted me to.

Well technically I made that decision for myself, but was under the impression I was doing what was best for my family. I was an emotional mess, because the very man I protected was the same man to cause me pain, and that was the turning point for me. I thought the Divorce was the end of this battle with him, and believed he did enough to try to kill my soul, but was I wrong. I realized that I was not dealing with someone normal, but rather a narcissist, that had nothing but time to mirror his feelings of himself upon me. A year ago, I decided to take him off the initial child support agreement because we were co-parenting with no issues. He would make comments about how he wanted to know where his support was going, so I made him responsible for half of our son's school tuition. If you have not endured Divorce, it is an extremely ugly battle between two people who once loved each other, that at some point turned into hate. Not always the case but this occurs for most. They say its a thin line, and to be honest, this is true. Our relationship thrived and blossomed during trauma, in our happiness we fought the most. We were two people who felt unworthy of life's blessings. When you're not married and have a commitment with someone such as a child, you don't necessarily have to involve the courts unless you cannot come to a mutual agreement. Once married, it is a requirement with the divorce process. A once intimate relationship that involved just the family then becomes the business of the court and the county.

As black women, I see on social media, women post their pride about not receiving assistance from their child's father. It is like that awards them as the mother of the year, for their independence and lack of support. I don't deny them of this, but realized that raising a child is not solely meant to be done alone financially, physically or spiritually alone. Now if the father is abusive to the child and neglectful, that is a whole other story. I decided that it was time to revisit this option as his father was not withholding his commitment to his son. I pay tuition, housing, insurance, and extra-curricular activities solely myself. For the past three years his father remained unemployed and would play the court system and me. It's unfortunate because there are fathers out there that actually are doing for their children and women take advantage due to their emotional baggage they haven't unpacked. However this is not my case. Today in my time loop he repeated everything that he has said in the past. The same lies and other spiteful things he usually says to diminish me as the primary parent. "She is mad that I don't want her that is why we are here." I had to chuckle to myself, because my only concern was I had fallen behind on my son's tuition payments with all of my additional responsibilities as a homeowner, and single mother.

I actually felt bad for him, because he is stuck. Stuck in the same space that I met him 10 years ago in which I thought I could fix. He appeared in all black, which was a symbol of the darkness that is clouding him. He never could give me eye contact because the child in him knew of the guilt he felt in his adult body. I provided every document required to state my claim, while he remained empty-handed with not a paycheck stub to be found. I used to get frustrated with the idea that I had to prove to the courts what type of parent I was. This actually is not the case. You see, when you do all things in love and are living life in your truth there is no need for proof. A blind man could read between the lines of every word that came out of each of our mouths. I have felt guilty so many years for his circumstances, and feel uneasy as he is a reflection of someone I chose years ago. I tried over and over again thinking that my son would only be complete with all three of us as a unit in the same home. I wanted what I did not in my childhood. So I did everything to make it work. A man on his current level today, I wouldn't give the time of day! It hurts to see that he is the very man I don't want my son to become. I feel for the black man, and all of his struggles. To a point we as black women and mothers are coddling some of them and restricting their growth. Some of us women stand in the way of their karmic debts and keep them at Groundhog Day while we suffer as the accomplice. I stayed with him for so many years, because I didn't want to abandon him like his mother. I eventually realized the love he was searching for could not come from me. He was looking for his mother to save him, but at this point he can only save himself. We are placed on this guilt trip when it comes to our men. We are to protect them and be their peace. What about the black woman? I fought years in court for his freedom. I think he forgot who was behind all that administrative work. Court dates paperwork, witnesses, and putting money on his books only to be standing with him in court to fight for what's right for our child. See, the girl years ago used to love this man more than she loved herself. Then she realized that she had to love herself more, not only for herself but to be a good mother to their child. I was the woman who stated she only wanted one man for her children, and believed that to be the right way. I no longer believe this is true.

As women we sometimes leave the door cracked hoping for the day that he will change, and that day may never come. I closed the door that last time he got close enough to put his hands on me. I pray for his happiness so he can become a better father for our child, and leave me the hell alone. Today, I found clarity outside of my emotions. I was even able to find him entertaining to say the least. I found it humorous that he appeared with the coat that I bought him. Everything I gave him he still holds onto. I no longer take what he says personally because he is fighting with himself and despises me for my growth. He can no longer curse me with his words because they no longer have value here. As women we worry about the man moving on and becoming the person he wasn't for you. Many times they don't change, they change who they are with. I feel for the next victim because who he chooses is a reflection of who he is today. I pray for her confidence, and ability to see clearly. Any man, who is willing to disrespect the mother of his children, will eventually do the same to you. I pride myself on advocating for my son and myself, even against someone I believed was family. Just a friendly reminder: It's not nice to make an enemy of someone who truly knows you, with my level of intelligence. A woman of my caliber is dangerous, and many are aware. People see your power, before you see it yourself. A little hood, but educated, and a heart full of gold. I'm not the type to start a fight, but when it comes to my son and his growth to become a well-rounded young black man, you're asking for war. It is beyond the money. It requires more than money to support the child, advocating for your child's developmental, physical, and spiritual growth is true child support.

APOLOGY...

I was given a $163,000 dollar apology for the negligence of the hospital for the death of my son. I wanted them to admit something I wasn't willing to admit myself. I neglected myself for years before they did. I had to split the money with my son's father, just because he was the father. I have been struggling to raise our son alone and even gave our family another chance. Everything that I ever worked hard for you benefited. You worked smarter not harder. You watched me sacrifice myself to the point I had nothing left to give myself, and you left. You left with pieces of me. Even after all the pain you have caused me, I had to share my blessings with someone so ungrateful. I had to learn that it is not up to me to determine another person's worth. I was your greatest actor, your picture perfect wife. I made you look good through my hard work. I always feared that I was making you better for someone else. Then I realized that I was the asset to our home. I made every house a home, was your confidant, and raised our son to be the young man he is today. I tried to force you to see that you were worthy to be loved by someone like me. I now see how much light I have added to your darkness and can clearly see how magical I am. Everything that happened to me has taught me that no kind of apology is greater than the peace of my forgiveness. No money can bring back my son, my time, or my sanity. The healing that I have done for over the past six years is worth more than any apology I have ever received.

MIRROR…

In every experience in life, we have to pay attention to the lessons it is teaching us. Our job is to decide on whether we are the teacher or the student. The true issue with today's society is that people forget it is our duty to teach or share experiences. It is a service. My recent experience made me acknowledge the test God required for me to fulfill. Let's just say I'm sure he is extremely proud in the way I handled it. I wanted to write a letter to my younger self as a way to kick off my writing a few months ago. Of course my procrastination took over and it has yet to have been completed. Instead, this weekend she was physically mirrored to me through my ex-husband's girlfriend. I never pray for pain or hurt to anyone and never considered myself to have an enemy. Even though my ex-husband had put me through so much pain, I never wanted to see him in pain or to suffer. We tend to think things or act out in ager when we are hurt and fail to realize that our behavior is creating the blueprint for our own Karma. Hurt people, Hurt people. This is a fact.

When you are on another level of understanding you realize the temporary fixes such as retaliating are not worth your peace. I knew from the day I spoke with her at the YMCA, I spoke to her soul. I am a firm believer in peering into people's eyes as they are the gateway to the soul. Her behavior and mannerisms said otherwise but her eyes showed me she was trapped. It didn't register to her that I once was her. The only difference was I was in this internal jail for 10 years. She was torn because she wanted me to believe that he "changed" for her. That something was special about her, and the flimsy foundation they built the relationship off was withstanding the storms. His and her pride could not let me see the reality. At one point, I believed he might have changed for the girl in the mirror and questioned myself as a whole. What was it about her that made him choose her? I played it very well for months maintaining my emotions. Faking it until I finally made it. I rebuilt myself and came to the understanding that my value was not determined by him not picking me. As women we want to be chosen, but realize upon being chosen, he wasn't what we expected. The girl in the mirror has a lot of similarities and her insecurities were highlighted because of how she got him.

I was the other women before. I believed that he was different with me, the only thing different is he didn't choose me. This weekend let me know I dodged a bullet. Never believe that what a man does to another woman, he won't do to you. If the man you are with is talking down on a woman especially if she once meant something to him, one day he will do the same to you. The girl in the mirror felt a sense of pride watching the man she wanted to pick her, disgrace and disrespect the woman he married. The funny thing is both girls want to be loved. We have dreams of having a family and being successful while settling for the picture he painted. We both loved a man who is incapable of giving himself emotionally because of his fear. I really dislike the meme that says a man will change for the right woman. I completely disagree and any real woman would not want him to do so. Any permanent change requires self-reflection, self-discovery, and self-love. When a man loves himself, he is able to love you. Changing for someone else is temporary, I tried it and it does not stick. This weekend God placed me in the fire to watch Karma unfold. After almost two years of rebuilding, healing, and creating a stronger relationship with God...he knew I was ready. I alarmed him and her with my sense of compassion, and empathy. I was not there to judge them or to say I told you so. I was there to comfort and guide the two very people that prayed for my downfall. The two very people that was entertained and enthused by my pain. I was resurrected! My purpose in life is to support and guide women through my own experiences. The woman that played a part in my divorce mirrored who I was years ago. So the moral of the story is before you go and pass judgement take a look at the bigger picture. It is not your job to react, be strong in who you are and remain yourself. It hurts to do the right thing. When pain is caused, it is human nature to react. I realized that what I had in store for those who had crossed me is no match to what karma they have built for themselves. The girl in the mirror may not realize it, but she saved me.

IT'S NOT ABOUT YOU...

Just because I'm being cordial, it's not about you. I have a higher sense of self-respect and energy that I try to maintain. My kindness is about me, and how I uphold myself. Every ounce of energy I waste on you moves me further from where I am taking myself. So you think you may have won, or you may feel secure by placing the blame on someone other than yourself. Whatever it is that helps you sleep at night, so be it! I fight with the old me every time I'm required to do what's right as opposed to what I think I should do. Every choice you make today determines your tomorrow, so I will fight this fight with grace. The internal battle is real as I feel your sense of contentment. But then I find peace in my strength and remind myself "It's not about you!"

HOPE @ A RUM BAR...

Jeremiah 29:11 "For I know the plans I have for you, Declares the lord, Plans to prosper you and not to harm you, plans to give you hope and a future." I had this scripture in a card that was given to me a while ago. When Micah was born, I cut the scripture out and placed it on his newborn photo that I had on my locker at work. I believe that signs are all around us and angels walking amongst us. However, I never believed I would meet one at a Rum bar. It was a typical Thursday evening that my son would spend with his father. I have become acclimated to trying new things on the days he spends with his father. This allows me to get back in touch with myself and learn more about the woman I am becoming. Most of my friends think I'm crazy but I do a lot of things alone. Anyone that knows me knows I wait for no one. I decided to head to this Rum Bar that just opened in a town close to mine. Every time I went with someone it was always packed, but when your alone you can always find a single bar seat. I was excited not just about the drinks, but I am also a "foodie" and extreme food critique. I cook extremely well, so it takes a lot for me to give good reviews on a new restaurant.

For the last few weeks, I have been going on this emotional rollercoaster with this co-parenting shit and there was nothing a little rum punch couldn't help. I sat down next to this Caucasian man who wasn't really my type, but he looked a few years older than me and seemed really nice. When you're single like me, it's important to keep your options open because Mr. Right is not coming to you the way you may expect. Your idea of "Mr. Right" vs. God's version of "right for you" may not be your "type". I believe any person that has a type is bound to repeat or continue in a repetitive cycle of dating the same people in different bodies. At this stage in my life, I need mental stimulation and after being deprived for the last 10 years, my mind craves it. I ordered my food and drinks but the waiter ended up bringing my meal before the appetizer. Service to me is everything but after my first drink, I was not bothered by the mix-up. The man sitting next to me noticed this and began conversation. Immediately, I noticed he had a wedding ring and thoughts began to cross my mind about his loyalty. Was he going to try to talk to me as if he is not wearing a sign of his commitment? Even if he did, at this point I have been blocking these types of situations left and right. Ladies, I know you seen the meme. God is not going to send you someone else's husband! We introduced ourselves through handshakes and he proceeded to tell me his credentials.

This man just recently got married to the love of his life after having a failed marriage of not even a year. He worked as an electrical engineer and traveled the world. It was so nice to talk to someone who did things or had things I inspired to have. He was on a business trip and he was staying at a local hotel and randomly ended up at this rum bar. He never once was inappropriate and spoke highly of his wife and their recent wedding. It's sad, but most of the married men/long-term men I knew complained about their marital commitment. Even though they were newlyweds they had been together for six years. I told him briefly my situation and he was astonished at all of my relationship trials and how I manage to do all that I do. To make a long story short after a few laughs, conversations about our future endeavors, and a couple of drinks we decided to go our separate ways. I am an extreme empath, so situations and people touch me in ways not everyone can experience. This man stood up from his chair to put his coat on and looked me straight in my eyes (something I was neglected of for years). He said to me " Whoever the man is that is going to come into your life for you and your son, is going to be one lucky guy. You truly are an amazing catch!" It may have been simple to the next chick, but to me I think he was an Angel! I wrote my list of all of the things I would want in a man, and he exemplified them right in front of my eyes. His professed love for his wife and love for himself. He knew what he wanted out of life and found someone who helped him in his healing process. Here at a rum bar, God reminded me that there are good men out there and that I was on the right path. Yes, I am still single after my divorce but I am preparing for our future. I refuse to settle and fall for one's potential. I come as a package and who I choose has to be a role model for my son. So I have to choose wisely. So that means I will have to wait. So just when I started to lose hope, I ran into Gods angel at a rum bar. He was an example of God's plan for me and his hope for my future. Cheers!

SPREAD LOVE...

Spread Love right where you are, just as you are! You don't need to be where you want to be, just be who you are. Our exterior and the way we portray ourselves to society, is just the icing on the cake. What makes the cake are the ingredients it took for it to become a cake. I am under construction! What you see on my outside doesn't necessarily mean that I'm as well put together on the inside. I have been physically and emotionally hurt, broken, and felt unworthy of love. Even in despair, the presence of love is always there. Spreading love consist of you giving of yourself. The most interesting aspect of this is it doesn't cost you a dime. In fact, giving of yourself is an investment. It is an investment to your own path and a seed for your future. What you reap is what you sow. Remind yourself that you are enough and everything you need is within you. Spread love through an act of kindness or a nice gesture. It is an exchange of positive energy that can potentially change someone's life.

LOVE FEARLESSLY...

Don't go through life just assuming someone knows how you feel about them. The anxiety you feel with the thought of expressing your feelings is the same anxiety they feel from you not telling them.

Love fearlessly.

THE CALM AFTER THE STORM...

When you ask for peace be mindful that some people may be removed from your space for a reason. It has been an eye-opening experience but enlightening as well. With my circle being so small, my decisions are made much easier and are based off of my own judgement. I spent a lot of time in the past asking for others opinions on my own personal matters, leaving me to do things others sought fit. Not anymore. I've been spending a lot of time on myself through working out and treating myself. I don't think people realize it but dating yourself is so much cheaper. I am attracting guys that like to court women and actually enjoy hearing me talk. My blood pressure is in control because at one point my body was constantly in the flight or fight mode. 32 is going to be a good age for me because I no longer need to apologize for me being me. I am who I am and if it is not fitting for you then you can dismiss yourself. Everything I asked God for I have received. My current position is not perfect but it damn sure is close. My path is clear! There are no trees, or rubble obstructing my path. I have jumped over hurdles over the years but nothing has ever stopped me in my tracks. I am learning to detach from outcomes and accept things as they come. Also I am constantly reminding myself that I am the prize and the gift for anyone whom I bless with my presence. This is for anyone that is experiencing a lot of drama currently in their life; ask yourself what role do I play in this? How can I minimize the confrontation? Who do I need to eliminate from my space? I will remind you that there is calm after the storm. You are in control of your space, but it requires some self-reflection to understand the cause of the drama. At one point, my life could have been a hit reality show (probably could still be but not a hit), something similar to Love and Hip-hop. It took me to realize that I am not that girl. Remove yourself if you love yourself. Invest that valuable time into something much more fruitful. Now I sit back and enjoy this calm after the storm!

MEANINGFUL GIFTS...

I am a giver and lover of meaningful gifts. If you don't know what a meaningful gift is, then you're missing out. A meaningful gift is a gift that is given to you or by you from the heart. It takes a lot of work to give someone meaningful gifts. You have to actively listen to the person about their desires and things that they love. You have to know the person on an intimate level, knowing them beyond the surface. I am very passionate about leaving my mark on people. I received a lot of things through my previous relationship from my ex but he was never the type to actually put thought into a gift. I did not keep any of the things he has ever brought me because they never had any value. What I mean by that is they did not come from a good place. Recently he returned the items he took from me as a way of bridging the divorce and conflict gap. He felt as though it was the right time to finally return items that rightfully belonged to me (this including my passport). One of the items were a painting he had got for me on a trip to Haiti to see his family. I always was intrigued by his culture and looked forward to the items he would bring back home.

This particular time we were separated but he thought to bring me an original piece of art made in Haiti. I love art and this particular piece was breathtaking. To be honest I truly think his mother picked it out because he never put much thought into his gifts. To make a long story short, I finally got the painting framed. As I was placing it on the wall, I began to really take in the art. I don't think he realized this but he gave me a piece of art that reflected who I have become. I am the strong black woman in the photo with her head held high. With the universe working in her favor. She is the universe. She is aware. Aware of what she was, and what see has become. She marches to the beat of her own drum. She is in control of creating her own paradise. That woman in that meaningful gift, in that unique piece of art is me. This said a lot to me about how I'm perceived, as opposed to what people say. Our divorce and separation was ugly but one thing he does know is my strength and my unique light. Gifts that are given by loved ones obtain their value through the thought that was put into the gift, not the price tag. I am not a materialistic woman, the nice things I want I can buy for myself. Meaningful gifts mean the world to me.

CELEBRATE IN SILENCE...

I am a very open person and love to share good news but recently I am becoming more aware of public celebration. I will use my son as an example as he is an innocent child. Every time that he gets something new or has something really cool he goes on a rant to all that will pay attention. Micah gets so excited to share with the world whatever new and exciting thing he received or accomplished. There has been many times where I had to shoot him down because his behavior could have been perceived as bragging. There is a fine line in this situation and all depends on the individual's perception. Micah, as I stated before is an innocent child and would be excited to share with others his happiness. It's unfortunate, the world we live in, because many perceive this form of celebration as bragging or boasting. The problem with some people is when someone else is celebrating a victory within their life; jealousy appears when the other's perceived "lack" is highlighted or magnified.

What I mean by this is the envy arises when the non-celebratory individual feels an area of their life is lacking. It is so important to monitor your energy in these circumstances because it can determine your fate. If you feed someone else's celebration with negativity because of your "lack" you will repel this from occurring for you. I always believe that when I see things happening for others that I am on the same frequency. If you remain positive, and trust whatever you ask for you will receive. As for those who envy because of the "lack" they will repel from their alignment of the receiving frequency. Things that we think we lack or don't have are frequently highlighted in our lives. For example, when you're single everybody and their mother are in a relationship and it appears to be a Cinderella story for them all. I remember having a breakdown after being separated for a year and unsuccessful dating. I broke down to my friends with anger about how much I deserved to be in a healthy happy relationship. Be mindful of others energy towards your victories. There are people out there that will wish you bad and curse the very thing you were celebrating. So from now on in my personal and professional life, I will celebrate in silence until my victory is set in stone. The very thing you may think someone is bragging about is potentially a highlight of your own insecurity. Just some food for thought!

INTERVIEW...

The beginning of a relationship and getting to know someone is like an Interview process. If you're like me, it can be very daunting trying to find a potential partner suitable for me and my son. Especially today in this social media ran society. When you meet someone they are showing you the best version of themselves. The goal is to impress you and to win you over through highlighting all of their good qualities. The dating process allows you to spend some intimate time with the candidate to learn more about them. Previously, I would not ask much and let things flow into the full-blown relationship. Only to realize at this point the person and I do not have the same values or similar interest. So since my divorce, I have made a point to inquire about the individual's desires, goals and expectations from the beginning.

When I dated at a younger age, I was fearful to ask certain questions because I was worried he would leave or suddenly become uninterested (those damn abandonment issues). Now at almost thirty-two I am confident in weaning off those who are not making a positive contribution to my life. I have a few strikes against me when it comes to this dating world. 1) I AM A BLACK WOMAN (dark skin at that) 2) I am a single parent 3) I suffer from the independent mindset because I did and do everything myself. 4) I own my own home and remain career driven. To anyone else these would seem like positive contributions to any relationship. Most men see it as intimidating, or maybe they are boys. I have come a long way to be where I am in my personal and professional life. I require the same things that I give to myself and within a relationship. Consistency is key! Take notes ladies when it comes to the dating process.

Make sure that his actions match up alongside his words. Everyone has a different interpretation of love. Find out what "Love" means to him. What was his childhood like, as this plays a huge part in how he views relationships. Now I see why employers require a 90 day probationary period for positions. It is required to monitor the new employee's integrity and consistency within their new title. You do well during the interview (the initial date) but once you get chosen your commitment to the position begins to slack off. Communication is imperative! Keep the communication open about your likes and dislikes and set boundaries and stick to them. Then you have the candidates that know they are on a TEMP assignment, because they never had long-term intentions with you but they reap the benefits of the permanent position. This is not okay! We are confusing good sex with love and not getting to know the person. We as women love to talk, but take the time to listen to see where his head is at. I refuse to give "Temp" employees my "permanent" employee's benefits. This is a top-notch company that requires a dedicated staff. My texts have turned into candidate rejection letters and the block option has allowed me to remove my emotions. I am not looking for perfect, I am looking for someone who finds me as one of their passions and is willing to bring us to another level. I have a lot to lose and am willing to take risks but only with the right candidate.

IN A RELATIONSHIP ARE YOU PRODUCTIVE…

I will be the first to admit, I think there is a purpose behind me still being single. For one, my expectations differ as I have aged. While we are constantly told to trust the process, many forget to pay close attention to the lessons within the process. I have learned that as time passes, every person you meet, and circumstances you encounter are pieces to your life's puzzle. Right this very moment, I have something that needs to be completed. I have something that I am required to do prior to being committed. When in a relationship, I make myself second priority. It's not that I won't accomplish things; it just takes a bit longer. I have accomplished so much within the last year than I have in my long-term relationship. Being a people pleaser doesn't help either.

In October I will be going on three years without a lack of partnership. The years have gone by so fast, but I have learned so much along the way. I wish I lived a normal life, but I guess I asked for this. My life has become one that is not just about abundance but of spiritual meaning and understanding. Most people don't even understand the world we live in. Every day I am given 24 hours to do something productive, something purpose driven. The first thing we say when we go through a break up is the amount of time we wasted. How we could have done this, or could have done that. In relationships we should not fear becoming or growing into our fullest potential. If you are in a relationship where you feel like you have to limit your growth that is not a healthy relationship. They are not watering you. A spouse should be supportive of any growth. Many times as women we are taught not to be an overachiever or to not focus on our individual goals. This is so wrong. Any growth within a partnership benefits both individuals.

A real man will not feel insecure about you crushing your goals. Instead, he will walk beside you proud while aspiring to do the same. We all see the videos of women talking about their "glow up" after a break up. Skin is clear, back hitting the gym, and energy and love frequency is on 100. That is all good, but if she is not aware, she will fall right back into the cycle. Falling in love, getting comfortable, lack of self-care, break up, and glow up all over again. For me, I am trying something different. I am aware of my lack of productivity, and make sure that I will not repeat this cycle. Pay attention to you behaviors and always remember never allow another person to dim your light. Shine girl Shine!

THE GUILTY MOM...

There is an epidemic that internationally affects women across the world that have children. It is a psychologically self-inflicted guilt when we engage in activities outside of our children. The guilt denies these women of their happiness, and distracts them from the activity they were to engage or supposed to participate in. Every other weekend, my husband takes my son to spend quality time. During the first few weekends, I drove myself crazy. I wanted to control things that even I wouldn't have control over even if he was with me. As time passed, I began to take the time to find new things about myself. I remember hanging out with some friend's family members, and I asked one of the "moms" to come out for the evening with us. She proceeded to tell me that she was a "mother" and that was her priority. Does being a mother mean to sacrifice your identity as a woman or a living being? Does the fact that I want to do something outside of my child make me less than a mother? The answer is hell no!. It's beyond going clubbing every weekend; it is a form of self-care. There is no need to feel guilty when it comes to taking time to get your hair done or a mani/pedi. It's even more difficult being a single mom feeling guilty being intimate. Mom's intimacy is important as well! Whatever it is you like to do or haven't done and would like to try...do it! Little did she know that made me a better mother. Just because you are physically in your children's presences doesn't mean you're emotionally contributing to them the best version of yourself. I always wonder do men feel the same guilt...sorry guys but I believe the answer would be no! Generationally the women before me have sacrificed so much for their children, which is typical and necessary, however it can turn into a point of resentment. I love my son tremendously, but I can't love him or show him what love is, if I don't love myself. Being an amazing parent does not require for you to stop living or being yourself. I no longer feel guilty for loving me.

OUR LIVES HIGHLIGHT OUR DEMONS...

What someone says about their life isn't always true. Most of the time, we shield our personal battles. We don't share the ugly but glorify the beautiful aspects of our lives. If you ever want to know the truth, take a look at someone's life they are creating. The personal demons we fight are highlighted through our daily struggles. My personal demons were highlighted through my son's father and his ex-girlfriend. Accountability is so important and we tend to forget that we attract people and our circumstances with our mindset. My son's father has issues with consistency. He never was consistent in our relationship and also to himself. I expected consistency from him but lacked it within myself. Not being consistent with my weight and healthy eating, my consistency to love myself. His shortcomings annoyed the hell out of me only to realize it was a reflection of how I was within myself. The disrespect and bad mouthing was a repeat of the things I have once spoken to myself. The things that bother you are there to teach you a lesson. Now his girlfriend, she really made me question this because she appeared to be the exact opposite of me. Her beliefs were different and lack of empathy as a woman really disturbed me. She was the woman that I could have been, and the woman I was.

I was the other woman but by me being "respectfully disrespectful" I believed bad karma would bypass me. No instead karma appeared as a young woman with two children and a vengeance. A young woman that could care less about being "respectfully disrespectful" and would fight for the man at any cost. She wanted to be claimed; she wanted love from a man. Her ways and words were that of anger and hatred. I never had the energy to feel that way towards anyone. The drama that was once in my life was a reflection of the internal demons I had to fight. I built bad karma and spent the last year by myself watching it like an episode of Power. I went from the student and became the teacher, now I'm on to the next lesson. Beware of your feelings towards your enemies and haters as they highlight your own internal demons. What angers you about another is a reflection of an issue within yourself. Pray for them to find their way.

TEAM PLAYER! BE CAREFUL WHO YOU PICK...

For my grad school class, I recently had to read a book called "The Five dysfunctions of a Team" by Patrick Lencioni. The book was for a leadership class that teaches the fundamentals of being in a managerial role. The book focuses on the corporate world and the five key principles for success. It is important for a company to create a team focused environment for the company to reach its fullest potential. With my vivid mind and interpretation, I felt like this concept of principles can be applied to not only the professional world but also personal. So, a lot of women are out here playing the victim when they have forgotten they played a role in their team building. I'm sure you recall being in middle school in gym class being able to select and build your team. Depending on the activity that day, you would point to the person or people you thought would help you win.

In certain circumstances you would pick a friend (knowing they weren't skillful), or how about the bottom picks (the last people to be selected). Most women, including myself have picked team players solely based of off their physique. The guy that stand 6'2 with the fresh-cut, looks like he may get the job done but has no skill or talents he can bring to the team. When it comes to picking players and when it comes to intimacy, the bedroom skills overshadow his life skills. You and your team-mate get pregnant and you're dealing with a lifetime of unnecessary conflict. This causing the main focus to be neglected and the child suffers. I once believed that love was what you needed for a lasting relationship. I now disagree. With love there are underlying components that need to be met. Whether you like them, or not, you are on the same damn team. I spent time in court battling with my son's father over custody. Although he was not presenting to me the dad I wanted him to be, he was an active father. I was stealing the ball from my own teammate. I don't care what no one says, a child needs both parents period. Fuck the "I'm independent" I can do it on my own shit. Unless the father is abusive or is a threat to your child, they need that time to build a relationship. It may not be what you wanted for your child, nor is it your job to discuss negatively to your child about this parent.

We are all learning day by day when it comes to this parenting thing. If you think you got it down pack, then your life must be perfect as well. Conflict is good, especially when you learn to argue fair. Learning the others behaviors and ways in which they communicate. Co-parenting means that as a team you have a common goal that also means going outside of your ego and needs. This was especially difficult for me because there was a lot of hurt on my end. I had to come to terms with his decision, respect them, and focus conversation on the bigger picture (our son). When it comes to picking a team member, make sure you have an accountability partner. I mean someone that calls you out on your behaviors, or things that are distracting you from your goals. At my age now, I am always surrounding myself with soul fillers, people who aren't afraid to tell me when I'm wrong. Stop surrounding yourself with surface people. There is no growth without accountability. In relationships with shared and separate goals, hold each other accountable so that the goals will become easier to obtain. Trust. Trust yourself enough to know that whatever trials may come to your team, that it will be okay. No team can always see eye to eye. However learning to respect and appreciate the differences allows everyone to grow. So ladies, that player you see with the light eyes, beard, and supple brown skin....check his stats. Make sure he has the skills and will be an asset to your team. Remember, you get to pick and build this lifelong relationship.

KILL THEM WITH KINDNESS...

Negativity needs to be fed for it to flourish. It is energy, and when ignored it can become powerless and cease to exist. Look at the negative behavior in the perspective of a child having a temper tantrum. The child is acting out using negative behavior for attention. If you react, you are feeding the behavior and the child will continue. Like the saying not every action deserves a reaction, be mindful of the energy you put towards it. It takes discipline and will power to ignore negativity, but it is possible. I have encountered many situations especially this year dealing with such circumstances. The best thing to do is throw them off of their own agenda. When you are aware of the fact someone is doing something with ill intent. In a kind way, you can throw them off guard by letting them know that you're aware and it doesn't bother you. The moment you show a sign of anger, you have lost. We all are responsible for our reaction and feelings. Yeah it may bother you that someone feels that way about you, but is that your issue? The answer is no! You grasp control of negativity when you remain positive. You don't have to own someone else's feelings or problems. Small minded individuals will view you not responding as a weakness. When they see you still smiling or being kind even after their failure to hurt you, this will make them reevaluate their approach with you. Sorry kid but throwing a tantrum won't work for me.

HELP....

Help! My brain is screaming yes, but my body fights the words that try to come out of my mouth. I don't know what has occurred in my life that I refuse HELP! My mother tells me it is the pride in me, but asking for help never seems to be the option. I am sure; I'm not the only one. I will be the first to volunteer if someone else needs it, but when offered, I immediately shut it down. It could be just the little things that may make life a bit easier. Like someone offering to take out the trash or even assist with the groceries. Yes, I am the one that will have ten bags in hand, determined to make it a one-time trip from my car back to the house. I'm even offered help even when it comes to work duties. I may have a lot currently on my plate, but refuse to receive assistance in completing the task. Is it really just to say that I did it all by myself. Yeah, doing things all by yourself is cool and all, but can be hell. I stretch myself thin everyday trying to be superwoman. It's true that you can't give everything 100%, but I damn sure attempt to. Only to end up disappointed. Why am I so quick to give, yet deny myself of any assistance from another? My girlfriend pointed out to me the very fact that unconsciously; I may believe that I am unworthy. I deserve to give but don't know how to receive. I am working on it. I now urge myself to allow others to do for me, as I have done so throughout the years. I am sure I have missed out on the many opportunities to receive what I put out. I will not deny myself the very thing I deserve. I don't need to prove to anyone my strength, and ability to get shit done. I will now kick my feet up and enjoy the benefits of someone willing to lend a helping hand. No longer will my pride answer for me. I still won't wait for others to get things done, but when offered I will take the help! Maybe some of these bumps along my journey will be a little bit smoother.

WHAT ABOUT YOUR FRIENDS...

As TLC would sing, or "Girl" by destiny's child, women it is important to have friends. Not just women but men as well, what would life be like without these encounters. I was told as a child by my mother that she would be my only best friend. I can understand why she felt that way because of her negative experiences with friends of the same-sex. Well she was partially correct; she is still and will forever be my best friend, even though most times we don't get along. I now understand that all relationships may not last, but they are experiences we are to cherish. We don't realize it but the people you call friends are what you have attracted whether good or bad. However, it is important to feed these relationships as your friends are those that make this ride of life more enjoyable (Especially positive ones). Some people consciously or unconsciously neglect their friendships when they become involved with a new love interest. I was guilty of this, and figured I would write about it as I see many women falling victim. We as women, when we fall in love, begin to focus solely on the relationship. We think the more attention we give him; the more he is supposed to love us right? Wrong!

I know from personal experience that I would constantly change plans for the one I was in a relationship with intimately. Forgetting and neglecting my relationships with family and friends. There is a saying that women go into relationship hoping to change a man, while men go into relationship hoping the woman doesn't change. I know in my head, I genuinely believed the more time I spent with a loved one the more invested and loved he would feel. This is wrong. It is all about quality as opposed to quantity. The relationship you are in is because the man fell in love with you for who you are. Who you are consists of your daily activities, goals, spontaneity, and lust for life. A lot of women, including myself, have given up those things and relationships solely to invest in their intimate relationship. Men love hard working women that are confident in who they are. You don't have to spend time out every weekend but once a month to get some you time with the ladies. I also learned that you can have your spouse as a best friend, but have your own lives.

Men are very black and white, so some conversations should be left for your bestie or a girls evening out. Not every woman in your life needs to be categorized as your girlfriend either. A true girlfriend holds you accountable and calls you on your bull. She is there to wipe your tears but not there to tell you she told you so. I have had many friends come and go over the years, not all were there to support me on my journey. They loved me at my worse and celebrated me at my best. These are the women that you don't forget, even when you're in a relationship. I recently spoke about this with a friend, how we are taught that getting the man is the end goal. Getting the man is the beginning but who you were before him and goals you had prior to him should remain.

Don't ever allow a man to stunt your growth both personally and professionally. If he has a problem with the women you hang out with it may be more about him, not them. They may be able to spot something your "love blinded" ass can't see. Not everyone is your friend, but true friends are hard to come by. I keep my circle very small, but make time for those that mean a lot to me, busy or not. It's almost August and fall is getting close. Cuffing season will been quickly approaching. My best advice to you is to fall in love, but don't forget about you or your friends. Love you first (God), and all else will follow. Don't forget about your friends.

IT'S ONLY THE BEGINNING…

Staring at the ceiling in my closet with the water stain, I immediately became frustrated. Just a couple of days ago, that wasn't there. The only issue is I can't call the landlord because I am responsible for this shit. I actually bought this home. Then I thought back to the frustration of the home buying process, and my excitement of being a homeowner. I was one of the very few in my family to own their own home. Where was that excitement when I looked at the stain, it had diminished. Buying the home was just the beginning, and I made a commitment to uphold my responsibilities that came along with being a home owner. Yeah you desire that car, body, children, and relationship/marriage but are you committed to the responsibilities that come along with it. The tangible aspect of achieving it and the emotional high that comes with obtaining that goal is momentarily. There is work that is required to be done to maintain the very things we desire, if we want them to last. That leak in my ceiling is a representation of my current foundation. A newly built home that represents my spiritual and emotional change. However the leak and where it is coming from defines some minor issues I am still seeking to overcome/heal from. A leak that is affecting me and unaware of where it comes from.

I dare not envy others for their situation or their circumstances. I don't know what it took for them to get there. Like my water stained ceiling, I am beautifully flawed. So once the excitement of the new job, big payout, or honeymoon phase light dims. Remember what you asked for comes with a price. A price that requires work to maintain, and a lot of responsibility. Be careful what you wish for...it is only the beginning.

TODAY I CHOSE ME...

For the last two days I didn't want to do a thing. My life doesn't allow me to take a time out, and mommy is not allowed an emotional break. I took a day off from work yesterday because again my energy has been drained. People have no idea what situations I have been required to face. People see changes within me but it's not just personal growth, I have been fighting spiritual warfare as well. My life and growth goes beyond the physical experience. I have been doing so much research and have been fighting between good and negative energy. Ten years ago, I married a man from a different culture. A Haitian man. Our cultural differences and genetic makeups set our relationship on rocky foundation from the beginning. The language and culture excited me, and opened my internal interest in the world around us. As time progressed I became aware of the effects of his upbringing and beliefs. I have said this in previous post, that as adults we are responsible for teaching ourselves how to reverse the wrong things we are taught. Although people may love us, the things they may have taught us may affect our very being. I thought that I could save him from the darkness. I fell in love with the innocent little boy within him. The boy who was not loved but physically hurt, the boy who was not fed. My internal light was dimmed by his darkness. My life with him was not normal, and me choosing to love him brought darkness to my life as well.

When we first met, he told me he was Catholic. Most Haitians consider themselves Catholic. However, voodoo is still being practiced within their culture. The flag they wave is symbolic to the practice and it is tattooed on his chest. The very ones that said they loved him taught him to dabble and make deals with the devil. Deals in which has affected his life and our life as a family. His blood runs through my son's veins. Now that I am aware, it is my job to save my son. His life is so dysfunctional but has become normal to him. The last few months, I have been brought to war with his demons. My sleep has been interrupted, and women I don't even know wish me dead. He was not living right, but I tried to show him otherwise. He became accustomed to the dark. The women he attracted practiced possessive bindings. Other women supported his life, the ones that benefited. Me on the other hand, I held him accountable. I wanted better for him. Better meant or required discipline and going against all he was taught. He made it clear to me today that he is too far gone.

Energy is real both good and evil. There is another level of life outside of the one we live. The last two days I was sinking into the darkness, the dark that I once lived in. My life was at peace because I did the work. The negativity I had encountered was not my own. I was being spiritually attacked, pained for someone else karma, an innocent bystander. Now that I am aware or spiritually woke, I will continue to protect myself and my son. Creating life is beyond the physical, and genetics. There is a history behind every individual, a story that will be written in your child's cards. God has shown me my strength is beyond the normal human level of understanding. I was called to not just save lives but souls. So many may ask why help this man. I married this man and vowed to be there through sickness and health. His spirit affects our child. I sacrificed the last ten years of my life trying to save his soul to the point that I almost drowned in his darkness. Today I chose me.

FEAR...

Fear used to live here but not anymore. Everything that I once feared, I've experienced. I used to be creeped out staying in the house alone but not yesterday. I came to realize that fear no longer resides within me. Everything I once feared has become a reality within my life. A reality in which I have overcame. I used to fear my truth. Fear others rejection. Fear the loss of relationships. The biggest fear was death. I no longer fear anything on this earth. The only thing that makes me nervous is dying from not living fearlessly. I have detached myself from the outcome and decided to focus on my output. I'm okay with taking risk, because the fear that once resided within me has turned into motivation. Fear feeds my growth. Fear is no longer my disability. What do you fear?

NATURAL...

A couple of months after giving birth to my second son, I decided to do the "big chop". If you're not aware of what this is, you must be sleeping under a rock. The "big chop" in the African American culture is cutting all your relaxed hair off, until your left with your natural hair. I decided during this time that I wanted to return to my natural curl pattern. It sounded like such a great idea and something easy to manage. This was normal for me because I used to cut my hair every time I was going through a break-up or wanted a little change. It seemed easy, but I had no clue how attached we women are to our hair. The first day I cut it and went to the jail to work for night shift, I hid in the locker room during road call. I already was tired of explaining the diversity of my hairstyle to my Caucasian male co-workers. They would always notice a change, or new hairstyle, and seemed to think I had this magic hair growth serum. This was when I was going between my natural length and 18 inch weaves. That night I did not want to explain why I looked like my newborn son, with about two inches of tight curls on my head. I knew eventually I would have to expose this new do, but I preferred to hide in the dark and listen to the inmates roast my new do.

For about a month, I tried to find ways to conceal my nakedness. I felt like I was baring my soul, without my hair being able to cover my ears. Time passed and my curls and length were in a not so awkward phase. I enjoyed flat ironing and seeing the true length. Soon, I was ready to be adventurous and try other healthy hair straightening ideas. I decided to hit a local hairdresser and get a silk press. A silk press is a flat iron, and a under dryer wrap that leaves kinky tresses silky straight and flowing. I didn't do much research on the hairstylist, but figured she was black and knew how to deal with my hair type. I was so wrong! After one silk press and twelve months on a healthy natural hair journey, my curl pattern was gone. No deep conditioner, or hair treatment could bring back a year of very minimal heat and gorgeous curl pattern. I was extremely disappointed but what I did afterwards was an example of lacking self-love. I figured since it was damaged that I would just continue to do so. All it took was one person to damage the progress I made within that year. I was finally where I wanted my hair to be and looking forward to the years to come. I sacrificed and dealt with some serious emotional attachment to something that never made me Kieona.

Similar to my natural hair journey, we as humans go through situations in life where one person or situation can occur that takes us off our path or goals. They can put you in situation where you have to hit the restart button. What about that diet and exercise you have incorporated in your life the last three months? You have been working so hard and one cheat day led to five. All the weight you worked so hard for you gained back. What I learned from my natural hair journey, is to not be so hard on myself. There are going to be some major setbacks when you make commitments to make changes. It's not the fall; it's what you choose to do after falling. If someone has hurt you and your heart was broken, is it smart for you to continue to allow others to do the same. We have a choice when the downfall occurs to either get back up, or continue to damage the very thing we allowed another outsider to do. To make a long story short, I plan on going back to my curls. The process is going to be a little easier emotionally because I plan on slowly cutting away the damage ends. It may take longer but this time around I will know better. Take it as a lesson learned, an opportunity to do better the next time around. We all have been there, failed school and worked harder when given the second chance. Maybe failed at the first marriage and learned more of what to expect for the next. My natural hair journey wasn't just about my hair. It was returning back to the very thing I once was. It was to celebrate the hair God gave me. It was about returning to my natural state. It was about returning home...

HAIR THERAPY...I SHAVED MY HEAD

November of 2017, my life was spiraling. I allowed myself to slowly fall back into my old ways by opening my life and home to my ex-husband. I became so frustrated with myself, as I spent so much time forgiving, and healing from the years of pain I allowed him to cause. I became weak, because the power that I worked so hard to regain was depleted within a span of three months. I fell into the role of wanting to be liked, and accepted. I became obsessed with being rejected, and wanted to prove my worthiness of his corrupted version of love. My vision had become clouded, and so had my judgment. I began to question myself and fought daily between the old me and the new me. With the overwhelming thoughts in my head, I needed to release his energy. I needed a release period.

I had been rocking a weave to maintain a versatile style for about two months. The day I took my weave out, I was amazed at the amount of new growth but had been frustrated with my curl pattern.

I just began thinking about the years of my lack of self-love. At that moment, I had the impulse to cut it all off.

I realized this was a reflection of how I felt about myself. My crown, my tresses are a part of what makes me a woman. This is something we pride ourselves about. Three years ago, I did the big chop and cut my hair to renew my curl pattern. It took one visit to a new hair salon, with an individual not concerned about my process, to damage a year and a half of progress with my natural hair. We can end up taking ten steps back on a journey through introducing ourselves to people not concerned about maintaining or aiding us with our personal journey. All it takes is one situation, one person, or one decision that can send you back pedaling to the beginning. Everything you worked so hard for appeared to be damaged within a span of seconds. It took me a while to digest the fact that after years of protecting my crown and nurturing it, I allowed someone to end up damaging it. Now, I know that those very setbacks are required. I realized not to be so hard on myself and to use what I learned for the next time. It unfortunate, because a lot of times, those very people who may cause those setbacks for you have no clue the damage they are causing. Those dead ends can be clipped, that pain can be released, and you can regrow and start anew.

My best friend and I sat around talking about the liberation in a woman cutting her hair. When I first cut my hair bald, she was the only one that I allowed to see me like that. The only other person was my son. I wish I could have video tapped his reaction and outburst of laughter. I couldn't help but laugh as well, but after, he asked if he could do the same. He said "Mommy I want to be healthy too." I knew at that point, I was making the right decision. As liberating as it was, I had to move past my ego and the insecurities in my head. I always wondered why when I went through a break up, or a life changing event did I have this desire to cut my hair. My best friend brought the answer to light to me today. She reminded me of the fact that she knew what I did before I told her. She said that when a woman cuts her hair, she is releasing the heaviness of her thoughts. When a woman is overwhelmed or consumed in her thoughts cutting her hair helps to release the heaviness, but doesn't rid her of her circumstances. She is creating a new foundation through cutting the damage and making room for new. When a women cuts her hair, she is about to change her life. Our physical bodies, and physical circumstances, are a representation of our thoughts. It is beyond changing her image and how the world sees her. She is embracing the women she is beyond her tresses. She is a rebel and is not defined by her hair.

My mother almost had a heart attack when I told her and could not understand why. To be honest, telling her was the most liberating thing for me. Growing up, I was taught to be everything else but myself. I had stripped myself of everything including intimate relationships, my hair, my brand new home, and so much more. I stripped myself of everything that others use as an illusion to distract them from knowing self. A lot of people fear that intimate connection of self, because there are a lot of hurtful truths we discover. It requires strength, love, patience, and nurturing. All the very things required to regrow healthy hair. Every journey is just that…a journey. To be honest, it doesn't end until the day we die, that is where the roads end. I am so proud of myself for removing the self-inflicted cancer of toxic relationships, and learning to love me, flaws and all. There is therapy in a haircut, because lately I careless of how I'm perceived. I have my days when I feel boyish because of the cut, and some days a complete bad-ass. My hair is a small portion of this whole being. I am beyond the physical as my personality and purpose confirms that. When I cut my hair I don't just change my life…I am influenced to inspire others.

INSECURE...

Last night at a Caribbean night club, I was moved by my purpose. I decided to take a trip to the ladies room to pat down my oily skin with some toilet paper. Ladies that have the oily t-zone area understand my issue. I wanted to check my makeup, and make sure that all the dancing wasn't catching up to me. My goal when going out is to look the same way I looked when I came in, especially when the club shuts down and the lights come on. When you find your purpose, you encounter situations and individuals everywhere that may need your spirit. The women's bathroom is a great way to connect with other women, especially at a club. I never thought to have the conversation at such an ungodly hour and while under the influence (of alcohol of course). There was a young woman in the bathroom clearly intoxicated. She wasn't hovering over the toilet but seemed a bit emotional. She was celebrating her 26th birthday and obviously she was having a blast up until she made that bathroom trip. She was standing in the mirror fixing herself up. I'm sure she had the same goal as me to keep up the look she had when she came to the club. Unfortunately, in the state she was in that would have been impossible.

She was dressed in a very provocative piece, a very short and see through dress. The dress left very little to imagination, and reminded me of something Beyoncé would wear for performances. She had bright red hair like Rhianna, and a curvy body that women would pay for. She was fixing her undergarments and exposing her backside. I kept praying that someone wouldn't walk in on the woman. At that point, she seemed to not care especially with her doing so in the presence of a complete stranger. Maybe at that moment I was a stranger, and her intoxicated state allowed her spirit to feel out my energy. She began talking about women's bodies and how we go through so much physically and mentally. She talked about how she was the mother of two children, both a boy and a girl. She explained how she had them both via C-section and the damage it caused her body. I told her that I had a C-section as well, and knew how insecure the damage had made me. Anyone that knew me prior to having children, knew I loved wearing two piece bathing suits to the beach. She was at the club with a love interest, and I had spotted them both on the dance floor prior to our bathroom encounter. Reality began to set in when she looked herself in the mirror.

It wasn't just her birthday; she was realizing that she was a year older. Every birthday most of us evaluate where we are, and how far we've come. We also recognize that in some areas, we may not be where we thought we would be. As she looked back and forth between me and the mirror, she became vulnerable and poured out her insecurities. She began to tear up and tell me how hard she is trying as a mother. You could tell she had been hurt by the men in her past, and feared the new love wouldn't last. Here she is a single mother of two children, insecure about her body, love, and life journey. I was there in that moment to reassure her, that she was not alone. I assured her that I too battled with insecurities with my parenting. We can only do the best we know how. I am reminded every time I stare in the mirror at my naked body, my experiences of childbirth. I struggle in love, and fear loving because of the hurt of my past. I know what it feels like to fear being happy in a relationship, because your waiting for the ball to drop. In that very moment, my spirit connected with a complete stranger to remind her that we all are insecure. We are all the same. No matter how beautiful, successful, intelligent, and strong we are, we have insecurities. Within a span of five minutes, both my business card and hugs were exchanged.

. It's beyond sharing a word, its inspiring others. To those who wish to do the same, to live in your purpose and inspire others, I'm the reminder that following your dreams doesn't mean you can't be insecure. It means that through all of your insecurities, and flaws, you're able to uplift others in their time of need. I am far from perfect, but through my mistakes, and life's lessons, I have been able to return faith in others when their faith has been lost. I am a living proof and a walking representation of resilience. Spread love through your insecurities. The best counselors are those with experience.

CLEAN SPACE...

Anyone that knows me knows that I love my space nice and clean. From studio apartments to becoming a homeowner, my living space is my sanctuary. A house is not a home without the energy that is placed in it. Before I bought my current home, and after my divorce, I redecorated my two-bedroom apartment I once shared with my son's father. This was important to me as I had to rid myself of the toxic energy we filled our home with. Love didn't live there anymore, but while I resided there, I made it a point to rebuild a new love there. I am the woman who doesn't leave to go anywhere without her home clean. Vacations, work, or just a night on the town, coming home to space and clear energy is important to me. My home decor and scented candles add the touch of serenity, and peaceful vibe. Depending on what visitors I may have had that day, you may even catch the stench of previously burned white sage. That's when I have to clear out the negative vibes. My window sill holds a rose quartz crystal that is placed directly in sunlight to invite a loving environment.

Every day it is not like this. Being a mother to a crazy, energetic four-year old, and all the other titles I withhold, maintaining this household can seem impossible. I manage, because my home is a reflection of my head space. When my space is cluttered or unorganized my creativity ceases to exist. I don't feel like myself. It's as bad to me as having the wrong outfit for a big event.

This week, my mother decided to come down to visit her grandson. My house was clean but it was not orderly. I went to the office as usual on Thursday and made sure I instructed her not to do anything while I was gone. We attended happy hour at a local restaurant with my little one in attendance. Micah was so happy to go to happy hour; he was looking forward to seeing some excitement. My poor child kept asking the waiter is it happy hour yet, he was disappointed when he realized he was unable to partake in the adult festivities. After dinner we headed home. In my home it is routine for everyone to take their shoes off. I have carpet throughout my home, so this maintains the carpet between the cleanings. I walked throughout the house to see everything neat and orderly. The house was not a mess before we left, but laundry and my room was always a bit out-of-order. My mother, who is not always physically well, took the time to make sure my house was just the way I liked it. I had to tell her how much I appreciated her help, as this was a gift that I truly appreciate. I don't ask for much, but when people take the initiative to do things for me without asking, mean the world to me. I had to express my appreciation for what she did, and told her how much that meant to me.

Her face lit up knowing that she did something to ease my busy life/schedule. As I walked through the house, I realized the symbolism of this very act. It wasn't about the fact she spent her whole day organizing my home. It was that finally my relationship with my mother was a clear space and at peace. You see, we never had a good relationship during my teens and early adulthood. The maximum amount of time we could spend together in a room without arguing was an hour. There was always so much tension and anger from the past that we just could not move past. I didn't understand her decisions and choices as a child, and she felt me voicing my opinion was a form of disrespect. As a mother now, I understand she did the best she knew how. Our relationship is not emotional and there is little to no affection. She explained to me her experience with her mother and how she tried differently with me. My grandmother was not the type to say "I love you" or hug and kiss her children or grandchildren. My mother yearned for this, but once she had her children she slowly showed her form of affection. My mother does say "I love you" but the physical aspect is very limited. As a mother, I am more affectionate with my son because of this. I had a successful week with my mother because I decided to change the way I dealt with our relationship. I forgave her for my experience that I had with her, and learned to accept her for who she is. Not the mother I wanted her to be.

When we focus on who we think someone should be, we bring more attention to their flaws or the attributes they lack. This blinds us from seeing the positive aspects of the individual. Her clearing my space was beyond organizing my home. She made room and space within my head and heart to grow. When we have these toxic relationships with loved ones, they can put a halt into our growing process, and limit our ability to love. She cleared a space that no longer is cluttered with negative experiences and resentment. I am able to view her as she is right now. My desire to change for my son, and his innocent love, has allowed a space for all those who love him to grow. We came together for one purpose, and that's to show and love this young black boy to the point where societies view of him will not validate him. Instead his cup will be filled with love, and his space will be clear to allow him to flourish to the best of his ability. If I were to die tomorrow, I would be content with the extent of effort I put into my relationship with friends and family. A lot of people leave this world with cluttered spaces of pain from their past. Not being able to say the things they wished they could have said, if only they took the time to clean their space

SECOND TIME STRANGERS...

This weekend, I made a spur of the moment decision to go visit family for the holiday. Such a great decision it was. I was feeling such extreme joy to spend time with such positive energy, my anticipation was overwhelming. This year I have committed to doing all the very things that make me happy, and what better way to kick off the year's transition with friends and family. With the New Year only hours away, the eve produced a challenge that I had no idea I would be confronting. I had a falling out exactly a year ago with a friend of over 15 years, which ended with a lack of understanding or resolution. I thought that at this point, I had accepted the fate of the relationship, until I was notified that I would be attending the same event with these second time strangers. The energy I had towards being in the same space after a year was charged negatively to the point I was ready to drive back home, from Massachusetts to Pennsylvania. After being made aware, I was frustrated with the lack of time I had to armor up energetically to not be emotionally attached to the outcome.

However, my frustration with the lack of clarification and resolution really did not allow me to ignore the "elephant in the room". I spent at least an hour trying to make a decision on how to handle my emotions, and make a decision on what was best for me.

I recently realized this with my hundredth time reconnecting with my son's father, that only through interaction will I see the progress of my healing and forgiveness. Healing in solitude is easy, but only through socialization will you be able to test your progress. With him I still have work to do, but in the case of the second time strangers, the chapter has closed. Within that hour, I created and acted out every possible scene that could have occurred. I planned on drinking during the event and was afraid my openness could create a physical altercation. That was not who I was, but who I have become is a person who believes everyone deserves at least me to remain cordial. After speaking to my son's godmother and her husband, they unclouded my perspective and really tuned me into making the appropriate decision for myself. Who I was, used to run from conflict. Who I am now stands in her power and truth by remaining true to who I am. I decided to stay.

If I left, I would be giving my power away. I guess it angered me that the length of time we were as friends that an understanding was never sought out. I guess I could have been the bigger person, but felt the relationship must have never really meant much to any of us. The reality is EGO stood in the way of both parties. I don't suggest this, but I drowned down three cocktails prior to the reunion. I had to kill the butterflies and expectations. The two second time strangers greeted everyone upon their arrival. The first says "Hi" with eye contact the other "Hi" with the side eye. The worst part was over and it was nearly not as bad as I thought it would be. The part that shocked me was the disconnect between my son, who they watched come into this world.

We are taught as children in school and by our parents to not speak to strangers. Beware! You don't know them and they can be potentially harmful. What about the second time strangers? The people who participated in your evolution, those you have given love and intimacy too. Those who once were strangers, then people you knew, and due to unforeseen circumstance, became people you did not know all over again. The night confirmed that we have grown apart, and also confirmed they may have thought they knew the person that I once was, but they were strangers to the woman I have become. In a year, so much has changed for all of us. One thing I was curious about was did she know the rose he gave to her for last Christmas, was my idea? That I reminded him that she deserved to be acknowledged that day. I know she knew because she looked at me that day as if she knew I had something to do with it. I played like I didn't, but I did. I guess at this point, I will never know.

Death has taught me the value of life and relationships. This year I have learned that not all relationships that end need to be reconciled. We closed a chapter that day in Disney on Christmas. New Year's Eve was the confirmation. I appreciate the experience and love I received while the years lasted. There are so many emotions that you experience in your encounter with second time strangers. For me, it was a sense of peace. For death has taught me to do the best you can, and give your all in your relationships. There is not one day that goes by that I don't let my loved ones know they are loved and appreciated. So next time you run into your second time stranger, just remind yourself they may have known you, but they have no clue who you have become, and give thanks to them for their participation in your evolution. My first challenge of the New Year was a success, universe bring it on, what's next?

FREEDOM...

I recall questioning why a woman experiencing domestic abuse would stay. I would watch a film or hear horror stories of women in emotional and physically abusive relationships. I always wondered what they were thinking. I always said that I could never be "HER". For ten years, I gave pieces of my power away, and created a debilitating cage of fear. I confirmed and made an agreement with myself, with every malicious or loving word that spilled from his lips. He confirmed the very things that I unconsciously felt about myself. I fed onto his promises as opposed to his actions. Until recently, had I broke away from the vicious cycle. I decided that enough was enough, and finally made a decision to do something for myself. I left everything I knew and worked hard for, all to escape to my freedom.

Last year, I purchased my first house around the holidays. A huge three bedroom home for just my son and I. This year, I became aware that I was living someone else's dream. Unconsciously, fulfilling someone else desires of me. I am currently sitting in a one bedroom apartment. I rented my home to make a transition and was told by the court and my ex-spouse that I am unable to relocate. That cage door has finally opened, but I haven't prepared myself to fly out just yet. I have seen the pain of one's life being in the hands of another from seeing my ex-spouse in criminal court. His fear of his freedom at the fate of bad choices he made and company he kept. He was at the point of suicide weeks prior to his sentencing. The stress of the process took a toll on him and made him aware of his every move. He really believed he was innocent and so did I at the time. At first, I felt like the victim. I did nothing illegal to deserve this treatment, nor have I ever had to answer to anybody about my personal life's decisions. My son was born in Massachusetts and was raised there until he was one. His father came around enough for me to choose "making my family work" and I uprooted us to Pennsylvania. No one questioned me at the time about my decision, except for loved ones. They saw how hard I worked in healing and making a life for my son and I. They showed a true concern for my relocation to his town of support. I asked God to make my family work, and he did show me exactly that. He gave me what I asked for, but showed me that the family could work, just dysfunctional and not how I would desire.

Fast forward, I am under the same stress while raising a five year old son. Originally I had thought to myself that he was trying to control my life, put a hurdle in the way of my goals. However, I came to the understanding that he can only get in the way if I allow him. I created this space in which I allowed his negative energy to block my dating life, professional life, and self-love. Those women I could not understand, I now do. They forget how powerful they are and fear cages them from flying to their freedom. The court system is slow and when someone's life is on the line it is better to play it safe. Freedom can be an ugly journey, but the only person that will fight for you is you. You have to save yourself. It all begins with the mind and moving beyond all the fears that block you from moving away from all that is holding you down, including a toxic relationship. It may take a while because your power was diminished piece by piece, but it is possible to regain. Once you have it, you will realize that no one can ever take it unless you give it to them. You will see that the cage door was always open, waiting for you to get the courage up to fly out. The court may have say over where I'm going physically, especially in regards to my commitment to my son and custody agreement. They however have no power over where my life is going, or over my dreams. He pushed me out of the cage and has forced me to fly on my own and for that I am grateful. He has reminded me of my power that very light he tried to dim. My freedom came when I changed my mind.

RESTAURANT...

Yesterday and today was another fight with the old me, and the woman I am becoming. I recently connected with an old "guy" friend, who I looked forward to hanging out with on my next business trip. I cut him off very briefly after inquiring "what are we?" around my birthday last year. My intuition had been kicking my ass a few times per usual, but I still refused to trust myself. After a few chats with the spiritual family and some thorough thinking, I decided it would be best for me to not reignite that flame. You would have thought I would have learned my lesson by now, but at least I am aware. As I have stated in previous post, healing is easy when done alone, but only through socializing will you realize how far you come. It is true, that if you want to see how something ends, pay close attention to how it began. I didn't realize it but my insecurities were written all over me. Also, being a single mother, boys playing to be men tend to flock towards us. Single mothers never really have the desire to take on the occupation of raising their child primarily alone.

I'm sure 99.9% of women would have denied that sign up. However, our desire for family and nurturing traits make us susceptible to attracting man-boys. They identify our immediate desire for family and lack of time for bullshit. So that means many of us are the "all or nothing" type. Sometimes our judgment becomes clouded because someone is finally just "showing" up.

So what the hell does a restaurant have to do with this? My spiritual family constantly reminds me of the law of attraction. I think it is amazing that I am on this evolutionary journey, but I get tired of over thinking and being so hard on myself. They reminded me that life is like a trip to a restaurant. In that restaurant, I can open this menu of unlimited desires and ask for exactly what my heart wants. Unfortunately, I am still the girl who is asked what would you like to eat and respond with "whatever" or "what do you plan on getting". Only to end up pissed off and unsatisfied with what I am served, and refuse to ask for something else.

My dating life has been like a restaurant trip. My first love taught me all the things I wanted and did not want. My marriage was the relationship that shot most of my desire rockets. Even when others treat us wrong, they teach us exactly what it is that we do want. After my marriage and my half ass healing, I went to the restaurant and ordered again and again. I am not a fan of red meat but like to enjoy a good piece of steak every now and then. I ordered steak every time at this restaurant because I had a taste for one. Each time I ordered there would be something wrong to the point I did not want to eat it. First time it was rare, second time medium rare, third time overcooked, and they all were exactly what I ordered. Steak. I never told the universe how I wanted it. There was times when the plate was nicely dressed and the food presentation was desirable. The taste however was not to my liking. Just recently, in my personal life had I finally had the guts to ask the waiter to take back my order. I mean I had all these weird ideas of what would happen or what they would do because I gave them more work. I would spend my hard-earned money and just accept things that were given to me. Not what I ordered or wanted. There is that fear of letting go of the what is given to you. I was told to appreciate whatever is given to you, but what if it's not what you've asked for. I feared that if I didn't entertain him, that I would miss out on the possibilities of what he could be.

He was good on paper, and good in bed. I can say that truly clouded my judgment, but is fifteen minutes worth a year of growth and development. Temptations got the best of me. I can't teach women about self-love and be a contradiction to it myself. So instead of the steak, I decided to say fuck it and go vegan. If I want something different, I have to try something different. Be aware that just because you have evolved doesn't mean that you will not continuously be tested. I have yet to learn to instinctively trust myself. With that information, how can I learn to trust someone else? We can't ask for others to provide to us the very things we are incapable of providing to ourselves. My next visit to the restaurant, I am going to order something that is market priced. Something that I feel I am unworthy of obtaining, In the meantime, my job is to continue working on me. Learning to not accept what is served to me unless it's exactly what I ordered off the menu of life. The great thing about life is that every day is another opportunity to become your best self, and to make another choice if the original choice isn't working for you. Excuse me waiter, I need to make another selection.

THIS TOO SHALL PASS...

I started the day off under the impression that it was going to be a rainy day. I already had it prepared in my mind due to my weather app, that we would be experiencing rain all week. This morning I woke up to bright sunshine and humid 80 degree weather. There were no indicators of a storm, so I prepared my son for the sunny day. My life has never been a dull moment and today was nothing different. With my couple of days off from work due to my birthday (my holiday), I was back to the grind like I never left. Bills, errands, finding solutions, every day as a single mom is a constant hustle. I got a few belated birthday text and provided some guidance to a dear friend. After my work day was completed I couldn't wait to pick up my son from school. One of my favorite parts of the day is seeing the smile on his face. Today, however wasn't a good day for him. In fact, he got into it with a classmate that has been frequently calling him names. I was originally disappointed of course and discussed his punishment as a result of the conflict. After having the talk about what he could have done better, I realized how much my son's day and one incident had completely shifted my energy. As I began to calm myself, I was able to actually hear him. Our children teach us so much about ourselves if we listen. They identify to us the very areas within ourselves that we have challenges. We get angry and frustrated over things that we don't even do ourselves. He began to cry and told me that he was sad that the other student had called him names. Out of his anger he hit the kid for calling him a baby. In his safe space he was able to be vulnerable and tell his mother he was sad. The sadness in front of the other student required an action to protect and defend his emotions...the sadness then turned to anger. I had plans to go to the park and usually would have changed my mind due to the situation that occurred. However I kept my agenda and told him to run and play to channel that energy to something positive. *I couldn't help but evaluate the many times I have seen acts of anger and took them personally, not listening or observing the underlying sadness of the other individual or myself.*

How interesting that tears can be formed with all three of these emotions anger, sadness, and joy. There is healing within that anger if we break down our walls to allow ourselves to feel the sadness. Within five minutes of play his mind went back to joy and at that very moment I envied his ability to shift his energy so quickly. 30 minutes in the park and the clouds began to change. There was a dark cloud that began to fill the sky, splitting both the sky with light and darkness. In the dark clouds there were very few spots of light. A lot of people see my work, see Facebook, Instagram, and think that my life is all roses. I am sharing, inspiring, and motivating even in my own storm. My days may start of sunny, and warm only to end up with a spontaneous storm. Some storms I can smell the rain and can feel the onset of the downpour. Others, I have no clue would occur and just patiently wait for the storm to pass. I haven't quite learned how to dance in the rain. I have learned to see the storms beauty and the importance of the rain. There is healing in water, and in tears.

Most days I am overwhelmed, stressed, and clueless about how I will make it through the next day. I realized the storms don't last forever. They can be destructive and turbulent but they are necessary for all growth. My inspiration and motivation comes from allowing myself to feel where most numb themselves. Being a parent is my greatest accomplishment, but the hardest thing is teaching another being how to see the beauty in the balance of life. I haven't listened to the real rain in a while. I usually watch YouTube videos of it to help me fall asleep. I am sitting in my car listening to the raindrops as my son rests. While I watched the storm pass as the roar of the lightening calms and the raindrops fall on the hood of my car. *I now understand while you're in the storm, it can seem very messy but from the outside looking in, the process from beginning to the end all makes sense. This too shall pass ...*

AMAZING GRACE…

Amazing grace is the black national funeral anthem. It is the most requested song that is sung during the funeral of a loved one. I used to cringe every time I would hear it as it always triggered someone to break down in tears of pain. Just recently, I was listening to some oldies and came across the Aretha Franklin version of the song. The song is about 8:00 minutes long but her voice was captivating. The song talks about being lost and found and finding home, but why do we need to do so during our transition to death. I do honestly believe that during our transition we are awakened with a new sense of consciousness, but why are we taught that we are only worth god's amazing grace at our funeral. I believe that situations occur within our lives that allow us to set out on the path in which we are intentionally creating the life we desire and are meant to have. We can become prisoners of our own heaven or hell through our perspective. Just by shifting our perspective of our circumstances can completely change our experiences. What if we were never "broken" or "lost". We never truly get off track, where we currently are is necessary to prepare us for where we are going. What if there is Grace within your darkness? If you search within, you may see its true purpose within your life. Losing my loved ones has taught me to live life now in addition to how to be fully present within the current moment. I learned to embrace the fullness of life. Home is where it all begins, and where your core beliefs are nurtured or neglected. When we leave the homes our parents have created for us, we have the ability to create our own homes under our own foundations. Through the grace of my trauma and my spiritual death, I was able to rebuild the foundation of my beliefs. I was saved by the amazing grace of the unborn life of my son London. Welcome home mommy is all I can hear! All this time I was looking for family relationships and people outside of myself to make me feel at home. All roads lead back to home. I have finally realized I am home, all with the help of a tiny set of footprints.

H.O.M.E

Now that I have found my way home, it is my duty to share some tools that I have learned along the way. I have created an interactive workshop in which you can use the additional pages provided within the book to document your own thoughts and emotions along your return home. Journaling/blogging contributed to my healing, and has allowed me to better understand and interpret my circumstances/current reality. Although our emotions are a huge indicator of our external circumstances, they can sometimes cloud our perspective and the actual experiences of others involved. I have broken down the word home into an acronym that can be memorized as a resource tool to provide guidance for those who feel lost within their transition. Home is not a place it is a feeling. It is a pure sense of love and joy that we always know we can return to. Many believe that this feeling is outside of them. However, this is an individual practice, and if done correctly can emanate and transfer to loved ones. That home feeling comes from all individuals under the same roof vibrating off of this pure love energy. The energy is what changes that very physical house, into a home. Home is a place that you can always return to, especially within the times you feel lost. A lot of people when they set out on their own believe they are going to find or reach this final destination of happiness. This is far from the truth. We set out to look for things, and become things that we believe will fulfill us. Only to find we have always been whole. There is no ending to any journey; however there are stages of progression and the evolution process. So while you are traveling on your journey, I figured I would give you some tools I found useful, and self-reflective activities that will give you a broader perspective on your current travels.

How many times have you seen a physically well put together home but the energy and people within it require some healing? Everything you see today is marketing and praying on the vulnerability of our society. Everyone is looking for something outside of themselves. I want to remind you that you hold the keys to your home…no one else. Resources, mentorship, and guidance should be free. I want to remind you to tap into your inner resources, intuition, and internal compass. Silence the loud ego, and be guided by the whispers of your soul. Remember that your journey is just a unique as your finger prints, and what worked for one person, may not be designed to work for you. These last few pages will give you the appropriate questions to ask yourself on this journey. Let your prints be your guide.

The H.O.M.E. breakdown…

H. HELP

This is the stage you have acknowledged you require some assistance. Something in your life right now may not be going as planned. You may feel lost and you see negative patterns that you are struggling to break. The first step in counseling or seeking some help is identifying there is an issue. Keep in mind (I had to remind myself this frequently as well) nothing is broken. You are not damaged, worn, used, or unworthy. Seeking help under panic in addition to believing you need to fix something is not the way to go. You have to learn to be gentle with yourself, and understand you are doing the best with the tools you were given. Now that you have the desire to want more, you are ready for the tools to begin your journey. Think of it as you are looking to move into a new place. When you are getting ready to move you search for assistance as packing and unpacking can be a lot of work. You need to find some movers or people with experience to help you settle into your new space. Think of this within a more spiritual aspect.

Ask yourself during this phase: What is my reason for the desire to shift or move towards the journey of finding home?

Am I doing this solely for myself, or for someone else? (Doing things for self are permanent decisions, doing things for other last temporarily)

What areas in my life require some improvements? (Home improvements)

When things need repair we call on professionals to assist us, what type of mentors or people do you feel can help you on your current journey?

O. OWNERSHIP PHASE

This stage was probably the most difficult for me and most likely will be for you as well. When you purchase a home, you become the owner of that property, just like you are the owner of self. It is extremely important for you to acknowledge that the very space you occupy whether physically or mentally you own. This requires accountability. There is power in accountability. When you take ownership, you are gaining your power back. You have decided to move out of the victim role, and to take control over the one thing you truly do control. YOU!
Ask yourself during this phase: Who have you been placing the blame on for your current circumstances?

How has playing the victim helped you to move from your current circumstances?

What role have you played in your toxic relationships? (Keeping in mind like attracts like)

The last question can be pretty tough especially for a woman who may have experienced domestic violence, the behavior of the other is not your fault, however your core beliefs of what you tolerate and deserve are the issue.

M. MOVING PHASE

The **M** stands for the moving portion. Packing and unpacking is required to transition into your new home. This is the process in which you have to consciously compartmentalize and let go of your negative and hindering beliefs. This allows you to make room for all things new. This is a tough process and requires hard work on your part. We have to pack away things that we need, and feel are important. Most of us don't discard the unnecessary memories and thoughts that we have been programmed with. Especially those they have been passed down generationally. Everything we have or hold on to is not necessary to bring with us to our next destination; this includes some of our relationships with friends, family, and intimate relationships. Also consider your dreams, goals, and how is everything including your job, contributing to making your soul purpose manifest. The more things we physically and mentally hold onto, the less room we have for new. Here are a few suggested questions to ask yourself:

What are somethings that you are attaching yourself to?

Do you believe that you may have issues with letting go? Describe these issues in details for you to review.

Does your living space reflect the very clutter that you have within your mental space? (Cleanliness is not just important for guest, but also is important for your mental well-being)

How often do you find yourself moving things from one room to another? What is the reason for you holding on to some things you may have mentioned above? What are your fears of letting it go? What do you think may occur?

E. EQUITY/EVOLUTION PHASE

Once you have solidified your reasoning to move towards finding home, unpacked, and have become comfortable within your new space you have now moved to the equity/evolution phase. You have officially removed the clutter and secured your space. Now it is important for you to remind yourself of your equity/worth. You have invested your time and energy into this process and gained new tools and resources that guide you on your path of evolution. It is important for you to secure your home space, as you potentially can fall back into old ways/behavior patterns if you are not careful. If this does occur remember that tomorrow is a new day, and a new beginning. Every day is your birthday, as it is another opportunity to be reborn. Within your new space be mindful of the energies you allow within your home. We secure our actual homes with alarm systems from intruders or thieves, but allow these very people within our personal space and bodies. Know your worth. During this phase ask yourself these questions to evaluate your new space, and what goals will you set for your next journey.

List three incidences from your past, in which you have allowed intruders or thieves to invade/contaminate your personal space? (Consciously and unconsciously)

Think beyond your old belief patterns and with your new found clear mindset, ask yourself who are you and where do you see yourself in your future? (The is no limit to what we can accomplish, think BIG)

What dreams have you let go of?

What are your deepest soul desires?

H.O.M.E is not a place it is a feeling. It is a feeling of completion and a state of being whole. Your relationship with self is the foundation that you build your home on. How you treat yourself will be reflected within the people you attract. A house is not a home without the energy of love and I was lucky to find that through the loss of my son. Become home for yourself...not home for others. The wrong people will abuse your consistent source of love, knowing you will always provide. Even when others are in the wrong, you will provide them a source of shelter. Be that for yourself. I am extremely grateful for your support and wish you continued success on your journey H.O.M.E. Trust yourself and the universe to guide you on your path home. Luckily, I had a small set of footprints that led the way for me. I am blessed to be able to share my experience and guidance with you.

"Welcome home mommy." London's Prints

We would love to hear from you. Please feel free to submit or upload your responses and comments. All information submitted will be reviewed as confidential information and will not be used for publication.
www.londosnprints.com
Londonsprints@gmail.com
Instagram @Londons_prints

ABOUT THE AUTHOR ...

Kieona Lenisha Renee Fairley was born and raised in Springfield, Massachusetts. She currently is a resident of Royersford, Pennsylvania where she raises her five year old son named Micah. She is a two-time graduate of Bay Path University majoring in Psychology. She currently works in Clinical Research will chasing her dreams of becoming a bestselling author. A graduate school drop-out, blogger, and dream chaser, she has found purpose in inspiring women through her writing and motivational speaking. She is an advocate for women that have experienced all forms of fetal loss. The author believes resources are limited to both physicians and grieving families on the healing process. On the journey of healing and finding self-love, Kieona has found the path of evolution to be as unique as our fingerprints. The author believes everything we need is within ourselves. The answers we seek, and the love we yearn for. Sometimes all it takes is a reminder. As for her, it was a tiny set of footprints.

39706126R00166

Made in the USA
Middletown, DE
23 March 2019